potato

potato

over 50 fresh and innovative recipes
for the creative cook

SALLY MANSFIELD

LORENZ BOOKS

For all recipes, **quantities** are given in both **metric** and **imperial** measures and, where appropriate, measures are also given in **standard cups** and **spoons**. Follow one set but not a mixture because they are **not interchangeable**.

Standard **spoon** and **cup measures** are **level**.
1 tsp = 5ml, 1 tbsp = 15ml, 1 cup = 250ml/8 fl oz

Australian standard **tablespoons** are 20ml. Australian readers should use 3 tsp in place of 1 tbsp for measuring small quantities of gelatine, cornflour, salt etc.

Medium eggs are used unless otherwise stated.

The recipes in this book appear in **Potato**.

First published in 2000 by Lorenz Books

Lorenz Books is an imprint of
Anness Publishing Limited
Hermes House
88–89 Blackfriars Road, London SE1 8HA

© Anness Publishing Limited 2000

A CIP catalogue record for this book is available from the British Library

Publisher Joanna Lorenz
Editor Felicity Forster
Design Wherefore Art?
Photography Sam Stowell
Food for photography Eliza Baird, Lucy McKelvie
Editorial reader Diane Ashmore
Production controller Joanna King

10 9 8 7 6 5 4 3 2 1

potato

introduction

There are **few** more important foods **in the world** than the potato. It has long played a vital role as the best all-round source of **nutrition** for mankind, and is now the **staple food** for **two-thirds** of the world's population. Potatoes can be **mashed, flavoured,** piped, mixed into pastry, made into **croquettes** and fried as **rösti,** and they can be used in both **sweet** and savoury dishes. They are **versatile** enough to form the basis of a simple **home-cooked** meal or to boost a special occasion with a more **unusual** dish.

preparing potatoes

WHEN IT COMES TO **ENJOYING** POTATOES, PREPARATION IS WHERE THE STORY BEGINS. THERE ARE ENDLESS **DIFFERENT** SHAPES AND FORMS IN WHICH YOU CAN SERVE POTATOES, FROM **WEDGES** AND BALLS TO FANS AND **HASSELBACKS**, AND COOKING METHODS ARE EQUALLY VARIED, FROM **BOILING** AND **FRYING** TO **BAKING** AND **MASHING**.

preparation

The method you use to prepare your potatoes affects the mineral and vitamin content, and the cooking technique.

CLEANING

Most potatoes you buy today are very clean, especially those from supermarkets and pre-packed potatoes, so giving them a light wash will probably be sufficient before boiling them. Locally grown potatoes, farm shop or home-grown potatoes may still have some earth attached to them, so give them a light scrub before cooking. If you are not going to cook them immediately, avoid scrubbing the potatoes with water, as they can start to go mouldy in warm or damp weather.

PEELING

It is well known that much of the goodness and flavour of a potato is in the skin and just below it. You can boil the potatoes and then peel them afterwards when they are cool enough to handle. The taste is fresher and earthier if they are prepared this way and the potatoes will be perfect for eating plain or simply garnished. Leave the skins on occasionally; they give more taste and added texture, plus vital roughage and fibre. Save any peelings you have left over for a very healthy version of crisps.

GRATING

Potatoes can be grated before or after cooking, depending on how you will be using them. They are easier to grate after cooking, when they have had time to cool, and can be grated on a large blade straight into the pan. Be sure you don't overcook the potatoes, especially if they are floury, as they will just fall to pieces. Floury potatoes are ideal for mashing, while waxy potatoes are a good choice for making rösti or hash.

Raw potatoes exude a surprising amount of starchy liquid that is vital to helping some dishes stick together. Check before you start whether you need to keep this liquid. The recipe should also tell you whether to rinse off the starchy liquid or just dry the potatoes on kitchen paper.

CHOPPING

Potatoes often need to be chopped for recipes such as salads and dishes using leftovers. If you are cooking them first, the best potatoes to choose are the waxy ones that stay nice and firm. They chop most easily when they are cold and peeled.

cooking

There are endless different methods of cooking potatoes – they can be cooked in ways to suit most climates, styles of cuisine and cooking abilities. However, the best technique depends on both the potato variety and the dish you are cooking. The following techniques illustrate some of the many ways you can enjoy this versatile vegetable.

BLANCHING

Potatoes are blanched (part-cooked) to soften the skin for easy peeling, to remove excess starch for certain recipes and to par-cook before roasting. Use a draining spoon or basket to remove large pieces of potato, but when cooking smaller potatoes, place the potatoes in a chip basket for easy removal.

STEAMING

All potatoes steam well but this gentle way of cooking is particularly good for very floury potatoes and those that fall apart easily. Small potatoes, such as new potatoes, steamed in their skins taste really delicious. Make sure potatoes are cut quite small, in even-size chunks or thick slices. Leaving cooked potatoes over a steaming pan of water is also a good way to keep them warm for several minutes.

SHALLOW FRYING

Use a heavy-based large frying pan to allow an even distribution of heat and sufficient room to turn the food. Heat about 25g/1oz/2 tbsp butter and 30ml/2 tbsp oil until bubbling. Put an even layer of cooked or par-cooked potatoes in the hot fat, taking care not to splash yourself. Leave for 4–5 minutes, until the undersides turn golden. Turn the potatoes over gently with a large fish slice once or twice during cooking until golden brown all over.

DEEP FRYING

When deep frying, whether you use oil or solid fat, be sure it is fresh and clean. The chips must be well dried, as water can cause the fat to bubble up dangerously. Always fry in small batches so the temperature does not drop too much when you add the food and it can cook and brown evenly.

ROASTING

Melt-in-the-mouth crisp roasties are what Sundays were meant for, so here are some pointers to make sure you get them right every time. For soft, fluffy-centred roast potatoes, you need to use large baking potatoes. Peel (you can roast potatoes in their skins but you won't get the crunchy result most people love), and cut into even-size pieces. Blanch for 5 minutes, then leave in the cooling water for a further 5 minutes to par-cook evenly. Drain well and return to the pan to dry off completely. Well-drained potatoes with roughed-up surfaces produce the crispiest results. Successful roast potatoes also depend on the fat they are cooked in and the temperature they are cooked at. Beef dripping gives the best flavour, although goose fat, if you are lucky enough to find some, is delicious and gives a very light, crisp result. You can also use lard. A vegetarian alternative is light olive oil, or olive and sunflower oils mixed.

MASHING

Ubiquitous mashed potatoes have seen a revival in recent years, transforming from a favourite comfort food into a fashionable food purely by the addition of olive oil or Parmesan cheese. Every chef and every trendy restaurant today produces their own version. It shows what can be done with a simple ingredient, but you've got to start with good mash. When choosing your potatoes remember that floury potatoes produce a light fluffy mash, while waxy potatoes will result in a dense, rather gluey purée that needs lots of loosening up. Boil even-size potatoes until very well cooked but not falling apart and dry them well, as watery potatoes will give a soggy, heavy mixture. Cold potatoes mash best of all. Sweet potatoes also mash well, to serve as a savoury or sweet dish.

soups

ROCKET ADDS ITS DISTINCTIVE, **PEPPERY** TASTE TO THIS WONDERFULLY **SATISFYING** SOUP. SERVE IT HOT, GARNISHED WITH A GENEROUS SPRINKLING OF TASTY **CROÛTONS**.

ingredients

50g/2oz/4 tbsp **butter**

1 **onion**, chopped

3 **leeks**, chopped

2 medium **floury potatoes**, diced

900ml/1½ pints/3¾ cups light **chicken stock** or **water**

2 large handfuls **rocket**, roughly chopped

150ml/¼ pint/⅔ cup **double cream**

salt and ground **black pepper**

garlic-flavoured **ciabatta croûtons**, to serve

leek, potato & rocket soup

method

SERVES 4–6

1 Melt the butter in a large heavy-based pan, then add the onion, leeks and potatoes and stir until the vegetables are coated in butter. Heat the ingredients until sizzling, then reduce the heat to low.

2 Cover and sweat the vegetables for 15 minutes. Pour in the stock or water and bring to the boil, then reduce the heat, cover again and simmer for 20 minutes until the vegetables are tender.

3 Press the soup through a sieve or pass through a food mill and return to the rinsed-out pan. (When puréeing the soup, don't use a blender or food processor, as these will give the soup a gluey texture.) Add the chopped rocket to the pan and cook the soup gently, uncovered, for 5 minutes.

4 Stir in the cream, then season to taste and reheat gently. Ladle the soup into warmed soup bowls and serve with a scattering of garlic-flavoured ciabatta croûtons in each.

galacian broth

IN THIS **HEARTY** MAIN MEAL SOUP THE
POTATOES COOK IN THE **GAMMON STOCK**,
ABSORBING ITS **RICH** FLAVOUR AND GIVING
IT A SALTY TASTE, SO BE CAREFUL NOT TO
OVER-SEASON IT.

method

SERVES 4

1 Soak the gammon overnight in cold water in the fridge. Drain and
put in a large saucepan with the bay leaves and onions. Pour over
1.5 litres/2½ pints/6¼ cups fresh cold water.

2 Bring to the boil, then reduce the heat and simmer very gently for
about 1½ hours until the meat is tender. Keep an eye on the pan
to make sure it doesn't boil over.

3 Remove the meat from the cooking liquid and leave to cool slightly.
Discard the skin and any excess fat and cut the meat into small
chunks. Return to the pan with the paprika and potatoes. Return
to the boil, then reduce the heat, cover and simmer for 20 minutes
until the potatoes are tender.

4 Meanwhile cut away the cores from the greens. Roll up the leaves
and cut into thin shreds. Add to the pan with the beans and simmer,
uncovered, for about 10 minutes. Remove the bay leaves. Season
with salt and pepper to taste and serve hot.

> ### cook's tip
> Peel the potatoes if you prefer, but the flavour is best with
> the skin left on.

ingredients

450g/1lb **gammon**, in one piece
2 **bay leaves**
2 **onions**, sliced
10ml/2 tsp **paprika**
675g/1½lb **baking potatoes**,
    cut into large chunks
225g/8oz **spring greens**
425g/15oz can **haricot** or
    cannellini beans, drained
salt and ground **black pepper**

> ### variation
> Bacon knuckles can be used instead
> of the gammon. The bones will give
> the stock a delicious flavour. Freeze
> any stock you don't use.

THIS CREAMY YET **CHUNKY** SOUP IS RICH WITH THE SWEET TASTE OF **CORN**. IT'S EXCELLENT SERVED WITH THICK CRUSTY **BREAD** AND TOPPED WITH SOME MELTED CHEDDAR **CHEESE**.

ingredients

1 **onion**, chopped

1 **garlic clove**, crushed

1 medium **baking potato**, chopped

2 **celery** sticks, sliced

1 small **green pepper**, seeded, halved and sliced

30ml/2 tbsp **sunflower oil**

25g/1oz/2 tbsp **butter**

600ml/1 pint/2½ cups **stock** or **water**

300ml/½ pint/1¼ cups **milk**

200g/7oz can **flageolet beans**

300g/11oz can **sweetcorn kernels**

good pinch dried **sage**

salt and ground **black pepper**

Cheddar cheese, grated, to serve

sweetcorn & potato chowder

method

SERVES 4

1 Put the onion, garlic, potato, celery and green pepper into a large heavy-based saucepan with the oil and butter.

2 Heat the ingredients until sizzling, then reduce the heat to low. Cover and cook gently for about 10 minutes, shaking the pan occasionally.

3 Pour in the stock or water, season with salt and pepper to taste and bring to the boil. Reduce the heat, cover again and simmer gently for about 15 minutes until the vegetables are tender.

4 Add the milk, beans and sweetcorn – including their liquids – and the sage. Simmer, uncovered, for 5 minutes. Check the seasoning and serve hot, sprinkled with grated cheese.

THIS SOUP IS **LIGHT** IN FLAVOUR YET SATISFYING ENOUGH FOR A LUNCHTIME **SNACK**. YOU CAN TRY GREEN **CAULIFLOWER** FOR A COLOURFUL CHANGE.

ingredients

30ml/2 tbsp **olive oil**

2 large **onions**, finely diced

1 **garlic clove**, crushed

3 large **floury potatoes**, finely diced

3 **celery** sticks, finely diced

1.75 litres/3 pints/7½ cups **vegetable stock**

2 **carrots**, finely diced

1 medium **cauliflower**, chopped

15ml/1 tbsp chopped fresh **dill**

15ml/1 tbsp **lemon juice**

5ml/1 tsp **mustard powder**

1.5ml/¼ tsp **caraway seeds**

300ml/½ pint/1¼ cups **single cream**

salt and ground **black pepper**

shredded **spring onions**, **cauliflower** leaves and florets, to garnish

cream of cauliflower soup

method

SERVES 6

1 Heat the oil in a large saucepan, add the onions and garlic and fry them for a few minutes until they soften. Add the potatoes, celery and stock and simmer for 10 minutes.

2 Add the carrots and simmer for a further 10 minutes.

3 Add the cauliflower, fresh dill, lemon juice, mustard powder and caraway seeds and simmer for 20 minutes.

4 Process the soup in a blender or food processor until smooth, return to the saucepan and stir in the cream. Season to taste and serve garnished with shredded spring onions, cauliflower leaves and florets.

corn & sweet potato soup

THE COMBINATION OF **SWEETCORN** AND **SWEET POTATO** GIVES THIS SOUP A REAL DEPTH OF FLAVOUR AS WELL AS MAKING IT LOOK VERY **COLOURFUL**.

ingredients

15ml/1 tbsp **olive oil**

1 **onion**, finely chopped

2 **garlic cloves**, crushed

1 small **red chilli**, seeded and finely chopped

1.75 litres/3 pints/7½ cups **vegetable stock**

10ml/2 tsp ground **cumin**

1 medium **sweet potato**, diced

½ **red pepper**, finely chopped

450g/1lb **sweetcorn kernels**

salt and ground **black pepper**

lime wedges, to serve

method

SERVES 6

1 Heat the oil and fry the onion for 5 minutes until softened. Add the garlic and chilli and fry for a further 2 minutes.

2 In the same pan, add 300ml/½ pint/1¼ cups of the stock, and simmer for 10 minutes.

3 Mix the cumin with a little stock to form a paste and then stir into the soup. Add the diced sweet potato, stir and simmer for 10 minutes. Season and stir again.

4 Add the pepper, sweetcorn and remaining stock and simmer for 10 minutes. Process half of the soup until smooth and then stir into the chunky soup. Season and serve with lime wedges for squeezing over.

minestrone genoa

THE **VARIATIONS** ON THIS SOUP ARE ENDLESS. THIS PASTA-FREE VERSION IS PACKED WITH HEAPS OF **VEGETABLES** TO MAKE A SUBSTANTIAL, HEARTY LUNCH WITH **CRUSTY BREAD**.

ingredients

1.75 litres/3 pints/7½ cups **vegetable stock**

1 large **onion**, chopped

3 **celery** sticks, chopped

2 **carrots**, finely diced

2 large **floury potatoes**, finely diced

½ head of **cabbage**, very finely diced

225g/8oz **runner beans**, sliced diagonally

2 x 400g/14oz cans **cannellini beans**, drained

60ml/4 tbsp ready-made **pesto sauce**

salt and ground **black pepper**

crusty bread, to serve

freshly grated **Parmesan cheese**, to serve

method

SERVES 6

1 Pour the stock into a large saucepan. Add the onion, celery and carrots. Simmer for 10 minutes.

2 Add the potatoes, cabbage, and beans and simmer for 10–12 minutes or until the potatoes are tender.

3 Stir in the cannellini beans and pesto, and bring the mixture to the boil. Season to taste and serve hot with crusty bread and plenty of freshly grated Parmesan cheese.

smoked haddock & potato soup

"CULLEN SKINK" IS A CLASSIC **SCOTTISH** DISH USING ONE OF THE COUNTRY'S TASTIEST **FISH**. THE RESULT IS A THICK, CREAMY SOUP WITH A RICH, **SMOKY** FISH FLAVOUR.

method

SERVES 6

1 Put the haddock, onion, bouquet garni and water into a large heavy-based saucepan and bring to the boil.

2 Skim the scum from the surface, then cover, reduce the heat and poach gently for 10–15 minutes until the haddock flakes easily.

3 Lift the haddock from the pan and cool slightly, then remove the skin and bones. Flake the flesh and put to one side. Return the skin and bones to the pan and simmer, for 30 minutes.

4 Lift the haddock from the pan and cool slightly, then remove the skin and bones. Flake the flesh and put to one side. Return the skin and bones to the pan and simmer for 30 minutes.

5 Mash the potatoes with the butter, then whisk into the soup. Add the flaked fish to the pan and heat through. Season. Ladle into soup bowls, sprinkle with chives and serve with crusty bread.

ingredients

350g/12oz smoked **haddock fillet**
1 **onion**, chopped
bouquet garni
900ml/1½ pints/3¾ cups **water**
500g/1¼lb **floury potatoes**, quartered
600ml/1 pint/2½ cups **milk**
40g/1½oz/3 tbsp **butter**
salt and ground **black pepper**
snipped **chives**, to garnish
crusty bread, to serve

CLASSICALLY KNOWN AS **HARIRA**, THIS SOUP IS OFTEN SERVED IN THE EVENING DURING **RAMADAN**, THE MUSLIM RELIGIOUS **FESTIVAL** WHEN FOLLOWERS FAST DURING THE **DAYTIME** FOR A MONTH.

ingredients

1 large **onion**, chopped

1.2 litres/2 pints/5 cups **vegetable stock**

5ml/1 tsp ground **cinnamon**

5ml/1 tsp **turmeric**

15ml/1 tbsp grated **ginger**

pinch **cayenne pepper**

2 **carrots**, diced

2 **celery sticks**, diced

400g/14oz can **chopped tomatoes**

450g/1lb **floury potatoes**, diced

5 strands **saffron**

400g/14oz can **chick-peas**, drained

30ml/2 tbsp chopped fresh **coriander**

15ml/1 tbsp **lemon juice**

salt and ground **black pepper**

fried wedges of **lemon**, to serve

north african spiced soup

method

SERVES 6

1 Place the onion in a large pot with 300ml/1/2 pint/11/4 cups of the vegetable stock. Simmer gently for about 10 minutes.

2 Meanwhile, mix together the cinnamon, turmeric, ginger, cayenne pepper and 30ml/2 tbsp of stock to form a paste. Stir into the onion mixture with the carrots, celery and remaining stock.

3 Bring the mixture to a boil, reduce the heat, then cover and gently simmer for 5 minutes.

4 Add the tomatoes and potatoes and simmer gently, covered, for 20 minutes. Add the saffron, chick-peas, coriander and lemon juice. Season to taste and when piping hot serve with fried wedges of lemon.

starters & snacks

potato skewers with mustard dip

POTATOES COOKED ON THE **BARBECUE** HAVE A GREAT FLAVOUR AND **CRISP** SKIN. TRY THESE DELICIOUS **KEBABS** SERVED WITH A THICK, **GARLIC-RICH** DIP.

method

SERVES 4

1 Prepare the barbecue for cooking the skewers before you begin. To make the dip, place the garlic, egg yolks and lemon juice in a blender or a food processor fitted with the metal blade and process for a few seconds until the mixture is smooth.

2 Keep the blender motor running and add the oil very gradually, pouring it in a thin stream, until the mixture forms a thick, glossy cream. Add the mustard and stir the ingredients together, then season with salt and pepper. Chill until ready to use.

3 Par-boil the potatoes in their skins in boiling water for 5 minutes. Drain well and then thread them on to metal skewers alternating with the shallots.

4 Brush the skewers with oil and sprinkle with salt. Cook over a barbeque for 10–12 minutes, turning occasionally, Serve with the dip.

> ### cook's tip
> Early or "new" potatoes, and salad potatoes have a firmness necessary to stay on the skewer. Don't be tempted to use other types of small potato, they will probably split or fall off the skewers during cooking.

ingredients

For the dip
4 **garlic cloves**, crushed
2 **egg yolks**
30ml/2 tbsp **lemon juice**
300ml/½ pint/1¼ cups **extra virgin olive oil**
10ml/2 tsp **whole-grain mustard**
salt and ground **black pepper**

For the skewers
1kg/2¼lb small **new potatoes**
200g/7oz **shallots**, halved
30ml/2 tbsp **olive oil**
15ml/1 tbsp **sea salt**

DIVINELY **CRISP** AND NAUGHTY, THESE **POTATO SKINS** ARE GREAT ON THEIR OWN OR SERVED WITH THIS **PIQUANT DIP** AS A GARNISH OR TO THE SIDE.

ingredients

2 large **baking potatoes**
vegetable oil, for deep frying

For the dip
120ml/4fl oz/½ cup **natural yogurt**
1 **garlic clove**, crushed
5ml/1 tsp **tomato purée**
2.5ml/½ tsp **green chilli purée** or ½ small **green chilli**, chopped
1.5ml/¼ tsp **celery salt**
salt and ground **black pepper**

potato skins with cajun dip

method
SERVES 2

1 Preheat the oven to 180°C/350°F/Gas 4. Bake the potatoes for 45–50 minutes until tender. Cut them in half and scoop out the flesh, leaving a thin layer on the skins. Keep the flesh for another meal.

2 To make the dip, mix together all the ingredients and chill.

3 Heat a 1cm/½in layer of oil in a large saucepan or deep-fat fryer. Cut each potato half in half again, then fry them until crisp and golden on both sides. Drain on kitchen paper, sprinkle with salt and black pepper and serve with a bowl of dip or a dollop of dip in each skin.

> **cook's tip**
> If you prefer, you can microwave the potatoes to save time. This will take about 10 minutes.

YOU CAN USE THESE **PINK POTATOES** TO MAKE SWEET OR SAVOURY CRISPS, AND THEY HAVE A LOVELY **COLOUR** AND A UNIQUE, ALMOST **FRUITY** FLAVOUR.

ingredients

2 medium **sweet potatoes**
vegetable oil, for deep frying
salt

variation
For a sweet version, sprinkle with cinnamon and caster sugar, and toss well, before cooling. You can prepare yams in just the same way.

sweet potato crisps

method

SERVES 4

1 Peel the sweet potatoes under cold running water, cut into 3mm/⅛in thick slices with a sharp knife or vegetable slicer and place in a bowl of salted cold water.

2 Heat a 1cm/½in layer of oil in a large saucepan or deep-fat fryer.

3 While the oil is heating, remove the slices from the water and pat dry on kitchen paper.

4 Fry a few slices at a time until crisp, then drain on kitchen paper. Sprinkle with salt and serve warm.

cook's tip
These sweet potato crisps are delicious served warm, but if you don't manage to finish them they are equally good as a cold snack. Serve with a dip, either sweet or savoury.

mini baked potatoes with blue cheese

PERFECT AS **FINGER FOOD** FOR A PARTY, ESPECIALLY AS YOU CAN PREPARE THEM **IN ADVANCE**.

method

MAKES 20

1 Preheat the oven to 180°C/350°F/Gas 4. Wash and dry the potatoes. Pour the oil into a bowl. Add the potatoes and toss to coat well with oil.

2 Dip the potatoes in the coarse salt to coat lightly. Spread out the potatoes on a baking sheet. Bake for 45–50 minutes until tender.

3 In a small bowl, combine the soured cream and blue cheese.

4 Cut a cross in the top of each potato. Press gently with your fingers to open the potatoes.

5 Top each potato with a dollop of the cheese mixture. It will melt down into the potato nicely. Sprinkle with chives on a serving dish and serve hot or at room temperature.

---

cook's tip

This dish works just as well as a light snack; if you don't want to be bothered with lots of fiddly small potatoes, simply bake an ordinary baking potato.

---

ingredients

20 small **new** or **salad potatoes**
60ml/4 tbsp **vegetable oil**
coarse **salt**
120ml/4fl oz/½ cup **soured cream**
25g/1oz **blue cheese**, crumbled
30ml/2 tbsp chopped fresh **chives**, for sprinkling

deep fried new potatoes with saffron aïoli

SERVE THESE CRISPY LITTLE **GOLDEN** POTATOES DIPPED INTO A WICKEDLY **GARLICKY** MAYONNAISE – THEN WATCH THEM **DISAPPEAR** IN A MATTER OF MINUTES!

ingredients

1 **egg yolk**
2.5ml/½ tsp **Dijon mustard**
300ml/½ pint/1¼ cups **extra virgin olive oil**
15–30ml/1–2 tbsp **lemon juice**
1 **garlic clove**, crushed
2.5ml/½ tsp **saffron strands**
20 baby, **new** or **salad potatoes**
vegetable oil, for deep frying
salt and ground **black pepper**

method

SERVES 4

1 For the aïoli, put the egg yolk in a bowl with the mustard and a pinch of salt. Mix. Beat in the olive oil very slowly, drop by drop, then in a thin stream. Add the lemon juice.

2 Season the aïoli with salt and pepper, then add the crushed garlic and beat the mixture thoroughly to combine.

3 Place the saffron in a small bowl and add 10ml/2 tsp hot water. Press the saffron with the back of a teaspoon, to extract the colour and flavour, and leave to infuse for 5 minutes. Beat the saffron and the liquid into the aïoli.

4 Cook the potatoes in their skins in boiling salted water for 5 minutes, then turn off the heat. Cover the pan and leave for 15 minutes. Drain the potatoes, then dry them thoroughly in a tea towel.

5 Heat a 1cm/½ in layer of vegetable oil in a deep pan. When the oil is very hot, add the potatoes and fry quickly, turning, until crisp and golden. Drain on kitchen paper and serve hot with the saffron aïoli.

polpettes

YUMMY LITTLE FRIED **MOUTHFULS** OF POTATO AND **TANGY-SHARP** GREEK FETA CHEESE, FLAVOURED WITH **DILL** AND **LEMON JUICE**. SERVE AS A STARTER OR PARTY BITE.

method

SERVES 6

1 Cook the potatoes in their skins in boiling, lightly salted water until soft. Drain and leave to cool slightly, then chop them in half and peel while still warm.

2 Place in a bowl and mash. Crumble the feta cheese into the potatoes and add the spring onions, dill, egg and lemon juice and season with salt and pepper. (The cheese is salty, so taste before you add salt.) Stir well.

3 Cover and chill until firm. Divide the mixture into walnut-size balls, then flatten them slightly. Dredge with flour, shaking off the excess.

4 Heat the oil in a frying pan and fry the polpettes in batches until golden brown on both sides. Drain on kitchen paper and serve hot, garnished with spring onions, dill and lemon wedges.

ingredients

500g/1¼lb **floury potatoes**
115g/4oz/1 cup **feta cheese**
4 **spring onions**, chopped
45ml/3 tbsp chopped fresh **dill**
1 **egg**, beaten
15ml/1 tbsp **lemon juice**
salt and ground **black pepper**
plain flour, for dredging
45ml/3 tbsp **olive oil**
dill sprigs, to garnish
shredded **spring onions**, to garnish
lemon wedges, to serve

GOLDEN AND **CRISP**, BUT **SOFT** WHEN YOU BITE INTO THEM, THESE **POTATO CAKES** ARE WONDERFUL FOR **BREAKFAST** OR SUPPER, WITH OR WITHOUT ANYTHING ELSE.

ingredients

450g/1lb **waxy potatoes**

1 small **onion**, grated

4 slices **streaky bacon**, finely chopped

30ml/2 tbsp **self-raising flour**

2 **eggs**, beaten

vegetable oil, for deep frying

salt and ground **black pepper**

parsley, to garnish

savoury potato cakes

method

SERVES 6

1 Coarsely grate the potatoes, rinse, drain and pat dry on kitchen paper, then mix with the onion, half the bacon, flour, eggs and seasoning.

2 Heat a 1cm/½ in layer of oil in a frying pan until really hot, then add about 15ml/1 tbsp of the potato mixture and quickly spread the mixture out with the back of the spoon taking care that it does not break up.

3 Add a few more spoonfuls of the mixture in the same way, leaving space between each one so they do not stick together, and fry them for 4–5 minutes until golden on the undersides.

4 Turn the cakes over and fry the other side. Drain on kitchen paper, transfer to an ovenproof dish and keep warm in a low oven while frying the remainder. Fry the remaining bacon and parsley and serve sprinkled over the hot cakes.

cook's tip
For a vegetarian alternative, omit the bacon and replace it with red pepper.

salads

IF YOU LIKE A GOOD KICK OF **MUSTARD**, YOU'LL LOVE THIS COMBINATION. IT'S ALSO WELL FLAVOURED WITH **TARRAGON**, USED IN THE DRESSING AND AS A **GARNISH**.

ingredients

1.3kg/3lb small **new** or **salad potatoes**

30ml/2 tbsp **white wine vinegar**

15ml/1 tbsp **Dijon mustard**

45ml/3 tbsp **vegetable** or **olive oil**

75g/3oz/6 tbsp chopped **red onion**

120ml/4fl oz/$\frac{1}{2}$ cup **mayonnaise**

30ml/2 tbsp chopped fresh **tarragon**, or 7.5ml/1$\frac{1}{2}$ tsp dried **tarragon**

1 **celery stick**, thinly sliced

salt and ground **black pepper**

celery leaves, to garnish

tarragon leaves, to garnish

variation
When available, use small red or even blue potatoes to give a nice colour to the salad.

tangy potato salad

method

SERVES 8

1 Cook the potatoes in their skins in boiling salted water for about 15–20 minutes until tender. Drain well.

2 Mix together the vinegar and mustard, then slowly whisk in the oil.

3 When the potatoes are cool enough to handle, slice them into a large bowl.

4 Add the onion to the potatoes and pour the dressing over them. Season, then toss gently to combine. Leave to stand for at least 30 minutes.

5 Mix together the mayonnaise and tarragon. Gently stir into the potatoes, along with the celery. Serve garnished with celery leaves and tarragon.

toulouse potato salad

WELL-FLAVOURED **SAUSAGES** AND FIRM **CHUNKY** POTATOES MAKE A REALLY GREAT LUNCH, SIMPLY DRESSED WITH A QUICK AND EASY **VINAIGRETTE**.

method

SERVES 4

1 Cook the potatoes in their skins in a large saucepan of boiling salted water for 10–12 minutes until tender.

2 Drain the potatoes, rinse under cold running water, then drain them again.

3 Peel the potatoes if you like or leave in their skins, and cut into 5mm/¼in slices. Place them in a large bowl and sprinkle with the wine and shallots.

4 To make the vinaigrette, mix together the mustard and vinegar in a small bowl, then very slowly whisk in the oil. Season and pour over the potatoes.

5 Add the chopped herbs to the potatoes and toss until well mixed.

6 Slice the sausage and toss with the potatoes. Season to taste and serve at room temperature with a parsley garnish.

ingredients

450g/1lb small **waxy**
or **salad potatoes**
30–45ml/2–3 tbsp **dry white wine**
2 **shallots**, finely chopped
15ml/1 tbsp chopped fresh **parsley**
15ml/1 tbsp chopped fresh **tarragon**
175g/6oz cooked **garlic** or **Toulouse sausage**
chopped fresh **parsley**, to garnish

For the vinaigrette
10ml/2 tsp **Dijon mustard**
15ml/1 tbsp **tarragon vinegar**
or **white wine vinegar**
75ml/5 tbsp **extra virgin olive oil**
salt and ground **black pepper**

the simplest potato salad

THE **SECRET** OF THIS POTATO SALAD IS TO MIX THE POTATOES WITH THE **DRESSING** WHILE THEY ARE STILL **HOT** SO THAT THEY ABSORB IT. THIS IS PERFECT WITH **GRILLED PORK**, **LAMB CHOPS** OR **ROAST CHICKEN**, OR FOR VEGETARIANS SERVE WITH A SELECTION OF **ROASTED VEGETABLES**.

ingredients

675g/1½lb small **new** or **salad potatoes**
4 **spring onions**
45ml/3 tbsp **olive oil**
15ml/1 tbsp **white wine vinegar**

175ml/6fl oz/¾ cup good **mayonnaise**, preferably home-made
45ml/3 tbsp snipped **chives**
salt and ground **black pepper**

method

SERVES 4–6

1 Cook the potatoes in their skins in a large saucepan of boiling salted water until tender.

2 Meanwhile, finely chop the white parts of the spring onions along with a little of the green parts; they look more attractive cut on the diagonal. Put to one side.

3 Whisk together the oil and vinegar. Drain the potatoes well and place them in a large bowl, then immediately toss lightly with the vinegar mixture and spring onions. Put the bowl to one side to cool.

4 Stir the mayonnaise and chives into the potatoes, season well and chill thoroughly until ready to serve. Adjust the seasoning before serving.

---

potato & radish salad

RADISHES ADD A **SPLASH** OF CRUNCH AND PEPPERY FLAVOUR TO THIS **HONEY-SCENTED** SALAD. SO MANY POTATO SALADS ARE DRESSED IN A THICK SAUCE. THIS ONE, HOWEVER, IS QUITE **LIGHT** AND COLOURFUL WITH A TASTY YET **DELICATE** DRESSING.

ingredients

450g/1lb **new** or **salad potatoes**
45ml/3 tbsp **olive oil**
15ml/1 tbsp **walnut** or **hazelnut oil** (optional)
30ml/2 tbsp **wine vinegar**

10ml/2 tsp coarse-grain **mustard**
5ml/1 tsp **honey**
about 6–8 **radishes**, thinly sliced
30ml/2 tbsp snipped **chives**
salt and ground **black pepper**

variation
Sliced celery, diced red onion and/or chopped walnuts would make good alternatives to the radishes if you can't get hold of any.

method

SERVES 4–6

1 Cook the potatoes in their skins in a large saucepan of boiling salted water until just tender. Drain the potatoes through a colander and leave to cool slightly. When cool enough to handle, cut the potatoes in half, but leave any small ones whole. Return the potatoes to a large bowl.

2 To make the dressing, place the oils, vinegar, mustard, honey and seasoning in a bowl. Mix them together until thoroughly combined.

3 Toss the dressing into the potatoes in the bowl while they are still cooling and leave to stand for an hour or so to allow the flavours to penetrate.

4 Finally mix in the sliced radishes and snipped chives and chill in the fridge until ready to serve.

5 When ready to serve, toss the salad mixture together again, as some of the dressing may have settled on the bottom, and adjust the seasoning.

cook's tip
For best effect, serve this colourful salad on a platter lined with frilly lettuce leaves.

warm potato salad with herb dressing

method

SERVES 4–6

1 Cook the potatoes in their skins in boiling salted water, or steam them until tender.

2 Meanwhile make the dressing. Mix together the olive oil, lemon juice, garlic, herbs and season the mixture thoroughly.

3 Drain the potatoes and leave to cool slightly. When they are cool enough to handle, peel them. Cut the potatoes into chunks and place in a large bowl.

4 Pour the dressing over the potatoes while they are still warm and mix well. Serve at once, garnished with basil leaves and black pepper.

TOSS THE POTATOES IN THE DRESSING AS SOON AS POSSIBLE, SO THE **FLAVOURS** ARE FULLY ABSORBED. USE THE BEST OLIVE OIL FOR AN AUTHENTIC **MEDITERRANEAN** TASTE.

ingredients

1kg/2¼lb **waxy** or **salad potatoes**

90ml/6 tbsp **extra virgin olive oil**

juice of 1 **lemon**

1 **garlic clove**, very finely chopped

30ml/2 tbsp chopped **fresh herbs** such as parsley, basil or thyme

salt and ground **black pepper**

basil leaves, to garnish

---

warm hazelnut & pistachio salad

method

SERVES 4

1 Cook the potatoes in their skins in boiling salted water for about 10–15 minutes until tender.

2 Drain the potatoes well and leave to cool slightly.

3 Meanwhile mix together the hazelnut or walnut oil with the sunflower oil and lemon juice. Season well.

4 Using a sharp knife, roughly chop the nuts.

5 Put the cooled potatoes into a large bowl and pour the dressing over. Toss to combine.

6 Sprinkle the salad with the chopped nuts. Serve immediately, garnished with flat leaf parsley.

TWO KINDS OF **CRUNCHY NUTS** TURN ORDINARY POTATO SALAD INTO A REALLY SPECIAL **ACCOMPANIMENT**. IT WOULD BE LOVELY WITH COLD SLICED ROAST BEEF, TONGUE OR HAM, BUT YOU CAN SERVE IT ON ITS OWN AS A **HEALTHY SNACK**.

ingredients

900g/2lb small **new** or **salad potatoes**

30ml/2 tbsp **hazelnut** or **walnut oil**

60ml/4 tbsp **sunflower oil**

juice of 1 **lemon**

25g/1oz/¼ cup **hazelnuts**

15 **pistachio nuts**

salt and ground **black pepper**

flat leaf parsley sprig, to garnish

> ### variation
> Use chopped walnuts in place of the hazelnuts.
> Buy the broken pieces of nut, which are less expensive than walnut halves, but chop them smaller before adding to the salad.

caribbean potato salad

THIS **PIQUANT** SALAD IS IDEAL TO SERVE ON ITS OWN OR WITH **GRILLED** OR COLD **MEATS**.

method

SERVES 6

1 Cook the potatoes in a large saucepan of boiling water until tender but still firm. Drain and leave to one side. When cool enough to handle, cut into 2.5cm/1in cubes and place in a large salad bowl.

2 Add all the vegetables to the potatoes in the salad bowl, together with the chilli, garlic and all the chopped herbs.

3 Mix together the cream, salad cream, mayonnaise, mustard and sugar in a small bowl. Stir well until the mixture is thoroughly combined and forms a smooth dressing.

4 Pour the dressing over the potato mixture and stir gently to coat evenly. Serve garnished with the snipped chives, and chopped red chilli.

ingredients

900g/2lb small **waxy** or
   salad potatoes
2 **red peppers**, seeded and
   diced
2 **celery** sticks, finely chopped
1 **shallot**, finely chopped
2 or 3 **spring onions**, finely
   chopped
1 mild fresh **green chilli**, seeded
   and finely chopped
1 **garlic** clove, crushed
10ml/2 tsp finely snipped **chives**
10ml/2 tsp finely chopped **basil**
15ml/1 tbsp finely chopped
   parsley
15ml/1 tbsp **single cream**
30ml/2 tbsp **salad cream**
15ml/1 tbsp **mayonnaise**
5ml/1 tsp **Dijon mustard**
7.5ml/1½ tbsp **sugar**
snipped **chives**, to garnish
chopped **red chilli**, to garnish

THIS SALAD HAS A TRULY **TROPICAL** TASTE AND IS **IDEAL** SERVED WITH COLOURFUL **ASIAN** OR **CARIBBEAN** DISHES.

ingredients

1kg/2¼lb **sweet potatoes**

For the dressing
45ml/3 tbsp chopped fresh **coriander**
juice of 1 **lime**
150ml/¼ pint/⅔ cup **natural yogurt**

For the salad
1 **red pepper**, seeded and finely diced
3 **celery** sticks, finely diced
¼ **red-skinned onion**, finely chopped
1 **red chilli**, finely chopped
salt and ground **black pepper**
coriander leaves, to garnish

baked sweet potato salad

method

SERVES 6

1 Preheat the oven to 200°C/400°F/Gas 6. Wash and pierce the potatoes all over and bake in the oven for 40 minutes or until tender.

2 Meanwhile, mix the dressing ingredients together in a bowl and season to taste. Chill while you prepare the remaining ingredients.

3 In a large bowl mix the red pepper, celery, onion and chilli together.

4 Remove the potatoes from the oven and when cool enough to handle, peel them. Cut the potatoes into cubes and add them to the bowl. Drizzle the dressing over and toss carefully. Season again to taste and serve, garnished with fresh coriander.

side dishes

herby potato bake

WONDERFULLY **CREAMY** POTATOES ARE WELL FLAVOURED WITH LOTS OF **FRESH HERBS** AND SPRINKLED WITH **CHEESE** TO MAKE A **GOLDEN**, CRUNCHY TOPPING.

ingredients

butter, for greasing
675g/1½lb waxy **potatoes**
25g/1oz/2 tbsp **butter**
1 **onion**, finely chopped
1 **garlic clove**, crushed
2 **eggs**
300ml/½ pint/1¼ cups **crème fraîche** or **double cream**
115g/4oz/1 cup **Gruyère**, grated
60ml/4 tbsp chopped mixed **fresh herbs**, such as chervil, thyme, chives and parsley
freshly grated **nutmeg**
salt and ground **black pepper**

method

SERVES 4

1 Place a baking sheet in the oven and preheat to 190°C/375°F/Gas 5. Butter an ovenproof dish.

2 Peel the potatoes and cut them into matchsticks. Set aside while you make up the sauce mixture. Start by melting the butter in a pan and fry the onion and garlic until softened. Remove from the heat to cool slightly. In a large bowl, whisk together the eggs, crème fraîche or cream and about half of the grated Gruyère cheese.

3 Stir in the onion mixture, herbs, potatoes, salt, pepper and nutmeg. Spoon the mixture into the prepared dish and sprinkle over the remaining cheese. Bake on the hot baking sheet for 50 minutes to 1 hour until the top is golden brown. Serve immediately, straight from the dish, as this will ensure that the potatoes stay really hot.

oven chip roasties

THIS **EASY ALTERNATIVE** TO FRIED CHIPS TASTES JUST AS **GOOD** AND IS MUCH EASIER TO COOK.

ingredients

150ml/¼ pint/⅔ cup **olive oil**
4 medium to large **baking potatoes**
5ml/1 tsp mixed dried **herbs** (optional)
sea salt flakes
mayonnaise, to serve

variation
Sweet potatoes also make fine oven chips. Prepare and roast in the same way as above, although you may find they do not take as long to cook.

method

SERVES 4–6

1 Preheat the oven to the highest temperature, generally 240°C/475°F/Gas 9. Lightly oil a large shallow roasting tin and place it in the oven to get really hot while you prepare the potatoes.

2 Cut the potatoes in half lengthwise, then into long thin wedges, or thicker ones if you prefer. Brush each side lightly with oil.

3 When the oven is really hot, remove the pan carefully and scatter the potato wedges over it, spreading them out in a single layer over the hot oil.

4 Sprinkle the potato wedges with the herbs and salt and roast for about 20 minutes, or longer if they are thicker, until they are golden brown, crisp and lightly puffy. Remove from the oven and serve with a dollop of mayonnaise.

cook's tip
Oven chip roasties make great mid-week suppers served with fried eggs, mushrooms and tomatoes.

marquis potatoes

A VARIATION ON THE **DUCHESSE** MIXTURE, FINISHED WITH A DELICIOUSLY **TANGY** TOMATO MIXTURE SET IN THE CENTRE OF THE POTATO **NEST**.

method

SERVES 6

1 Peel and cut the potatoes into small chunks, boil in lightly salted water for 20 minutes or until very tender. Meanwhile, blanch the tomatoes in boiling water and then plunge into a bowl of cold water. Peel the skins and then scoop the seeds out. Chop the tomato flesh.

2 Heat the olive oil in a large frying pan and fry the shallots for 2 minutes stirring continuously. Add the chopped tomatoes to the pan and fry for a further 10 minutes until the moisture has evaporated. Set aside.

3 Drain the potatoes through a colander, return to the pan and allow the steam to dry off. Cool slightly and mash well with the butter and two of the egg yolks and the milk. Season with salt and ground black pepper.

4 Grease a baking sheet. Spoon the potato into a piping bag fitted with a medium star nozzle. Pipe six oval nests on to the baking sheet. Beat the remaining egg with a little water and carefully brush over the potato. Grill for 5 minutes or until golden.

5 Spoon the tomato mixture inside the nests and top with a little parsley. Serve them immediately.

ingredients

900g/2 lb **floury potatoes**
450g/1lb ripe **tomatoes**
15ml/1tbsp **olive oil**
2 **shallots**, finely chopped
25g/1oz/2 tbsp **butter**
3 **egg yolks**
60ml/4 tbsp **milk**
chopped fresh **parsley**, to garnish
sea salt and ground **black pepper**

A POTATO DISH
WITH A **DIFFERENCE**.
THE TOP OF THE
POTATOES WILL
BE **CRISPY** WITH
A **SOFTLY** COOKED
BASE IN THE STOCK,
ONIONS AND **BACON**.

ingredients

900g/2lb **maincrop potatoes**

25g/1oz/2 tbsp **butter**

1 **onion**, finely chopped

115g/4oz **unsmoked streaky**
   bacon, rinds removed

350ml/12fl oz /1½ cups
   vegetable stock

chopped **parsley**, to garnish

sea salt and ground **black**
   pepper

berrichonne potatoes

method

SERVES 6

1 Preheat the oven to 200°C/400°F/Gas 6. Peel the potatoes and trim them into barrel shapes. Leave the potatoes to stand in a bowl of cold water.

2 Melt the butter in a frying pan. Add the onions, stir and cover with a lid. Cook for 2–3 minutes, until they are soft but not brown.

3 Chop the bacon and add to the onions, cover and cook for 2 minutes.

4 Spoon the onion mixture into the base of a 1.5 litres/2½ pints/6¼ cup rectangular shallow ovenproof dish. Lay the potatoes over the onion mixture and pour the stock over, making sure that it comes halfway up the sides of them. Season and cook for 1 hour. Garnish with chopped parsley.

hash browns

CRISPY **GOLDEN WEDGES** OF POTATOES, "HASHED" UP WITH A LITTLE ONION, ARE A FAVOURITE AMERICAN **BREAKFAST** DISH, BUT TASTE **DELICIOUS** ANYTIME.

ingredients

60ml/4 tbsp **sunflower**
  or **olive oil**
450g/1lb cooked **potatoes**,
  diced or grated

1 small **onion**, chopped
salt and ground **black pepper**
chives, to garnish
tomato sauce, to serve

method

SERVES 4–6

1 Heat the oil in a large heavy-based frying pan until very hot. Add the potatoes in a single layer. Scatter the onion on top and season well.

2 Cook on a medium heat, pressing down on the potatoes with a spoon or spatula to squash them together.

3 When the potatoes are nicely browned underneath, turn them over in sections with a spatula and fry until the other side is golden brown and lightly crispy, pressing them down again.

4 Serve hot with a garnish of chives and tomato sauce alongside.

variation
Turn this side dish into a main meal by adding other ingredients to the potatoes in the pan, such as cooked diced meat, sliced sausages or even corned beef for a northern English corned beef hash supper.

spanish chilli potatoes

THE NAME OF THIS **SPANISH** TAPAS DISH, "**PATATAS BRAVAS**", MEANS FIERCELY HOT POTATOES, BUT LUCKILY .**TAPAS** ARE USUALLY ONLY EATEN IN SMALL QUANTITIES!

ingredients

900g/2lb small **new** or **salad**
  potatoes
60ml/4 tbsp **olive oil**
1 **onion**, finely chopped
2 **garlic cloves**, crushed
15ml/1 tbsp **tomato paste**
200g/7oz can chopped **tomatoes**
15ml/1 tbsp **red wine vinegar**
2–3 small **dried red chillies**,
  seeded and finely chopped,
  or 5–10ml/1–2 tsp hot **chilli**
  powder

5ml/1 tsp **paprika**
salt and ground **black pepper**
1 **flat leaf parsley** sprig, to
  garnish
chopped fresh **red chillies**, to
  garnish

method

SERVES 4

1 Cook the potatoes in their skins in boiling water for 10–12 minutes until just tender. Drain well and leave to cool, then cut in half and reserve.

2 Heat the oil in a large pan and add the onion and garlic. Fry them gently for 5–6 minutes until just softened. Stir in the tomato paste, tomatoes, vinegar, chillies or chilli powder and paprika and simmer for about 5 minutes.

3 Stir the potatoes into the sauce mixture until well coated. Cover and simmer gently for 8–10 minutes until the potatoes are tender.

4 Season the potatoes well and transfer to a warmed serving dish. Serve at once, garnished with a sprig of flat leaf parsley. To make the dish even hotter, add a garnish of chopped fresh red chillies.

cook's tip
If you don't like your potatoes to be too fierce simply reduce the amount of chilli to taste.

potato latkes

LATKES ARE TRADITIONAL **JEWISH** POTATO PANCAKES, FRIED UNTIL GOLDEN AND **CRISP** AND SERVED WITH **HOT SALT BEEF** OR **APPLE SAUCE** AND **SOURED CREAM**.

method

SERVES 4

1 Coarsely grate the potatoes and the onion. Put them in a large colander but don't rinse them. Press them down, squeezing out as much of the thick starchy liquid as possible. Transfer the potato mixture to a bowl.

2 Immediately stir in the beaten egg. Add the matzo meal, stirring gently to mix. Season with salt and plenty of pepper.

3 Heat a 1cm/½in layer of oil in a heavy-based frying pan for a few minutes (test it by throwing in a small piece of bread – it should sizzle). Take a spoonful of the potato mixture and lower it carefully into the oil. Continue adding spoonfuls, leaving space between each one.

4 Flatten the pancakes slightly with the back of a spoon. Fry for a few minutes until the latkes are golden brown on the underside, carefully turn them over and continue frying until golden brown.

5 Drain the latkes on kitchen paper, then transfer to an ovenproof serving dish and keep warm in a low oven while frying the remainder. Serve hot.

ingredients

2 medium **floury potatoes**

1 **onion**

1 large **egg**, beaten

30ml/2 tbsp medium-ground **matzo meal**

vegetable oil, for frying

salt and ground **black pepper**

cook's tip
Try using equal quantities of potatoes and Jerusalem artichokes for a really distinct flavour.

TRADITIONAL **INDIAN** SPICES – MUSTARD SEED, GINGER AND **CHILLI** – GIVE A REALLY GOOD **KICK** TO POTATOES AND **SPINACH** IN THIS DELICIOUS AND **AUTHENTIC** CURRY.

ingredients

450g/1lb **spinach**
30ml/2 tbsp **vegetable oil**
5ml/1 tsp **black mustard seeds**
1 **onion**, thinly sliced
2 **garlic cloves**, crushed
2.5cm/1in piece **root ginger**,
   finely chopped
675g/1½lb firm **potatoes**,
   cut into 2.5cm/1in chunks
5ml/1 tsp **chilli powder**
5ml/1 tsp **salt**
120ml/4fl oz/½ cup **water**

aloo saag

method   SERVES 6

1 Blanch the spinach in boiling water for 3–4 minutes.

2 Drain the spinach thoroughly and leave to cool. When it is cool enough to handle, use your hands to squeeze out any remaining liquid.

3 Heat the oil in a large saucepan and fry the mustard seeds for 2 minutes, stirring, until they begin to splutter.

4 Add the onion, garlic and ginger and fry for 5 minutes, stirring.

5 Stir in the potatoes, chilli powder, salt and water and cook for 8 minutes, stirring occasionally.

6 Finally, add the spinach to the pan. Cover and simmer for 10–15 minutes until the spinach is cooked and the potatoes are tender. Serve hot.

cook's tip
To make certain that the spinach is dry, put it in a clean tea towel, roll up tightly and squeeze gently to remove any excess liquid. Choose a firm waxy variety of potato or a salad potato so the pieces do not break up during cooking.

straw potato cake

THIS IS **DELICIOUS** AS A **SIDE DISH** OR CAN
BE A **MEAL** IN ITSELF.

ingredients

450g/1lb firm **baking potatoes**
25ml/1½ tbsp **butter**, melted
15ml/1 tbsp **vegetable oil**
salt and ground **black pepper**

cook's tip
Another nice way to serve this dish is to make several small cakes instead
of a large one. They will not take quite so long to cook, so follow the method
as for the large cake, but adjust the cooking time accordingly.

method
SERVES 4

1 Peel and grate the potatoes, then toss with melted butter and season.

2 Heat the oil in a large heavy-based frying pan. Add the potato and press
down to form an even layer that covers the base of the pan. Cook over
a medium heat for 7–10 minutes until the base is well browned.

3 Loosen the cake if it has stuck to the bottom by shaking the pan or
running a knife under it.

4 To turn the cake, invert a large baking tray over the frying pan and,
holding it tightly against the pan, turn them both over together. Lift
off the frying pan, return it to the heat and add a little more oil if it
looks dry. Slide the potato cake back into the frying pan, browned
side uppermost, and continue cooking until the underside is crisp
and golden.

5 Serve the cake hot, cut into individual wedges.

sautéed potatoes

THESE **ROSEMARY-SCENTED**, CRISP
GOLDEN POTATOES ARE A FAVOURITE
IN MANY **FRENCH** HOUSEHOLDS.

ingredients

1.3kg/3lb firm **baking potatoes**
60–90ml/4–6 tbsp **oil**, **bacon**
   dripping or **clarified butter**
2 **rosemary sprigs**, leaves
   chopped
salt and ground **black pepper**

method
SERVES 6

1 Peel and cut the potatoes into 2.5cm/1in slices.

2 Place the slices in a bowl of cold water and soak for 10 minutes.
Drain, rinse and drain again, then pat dry.

3 In a large heavy-based frying pan, heat 60ml/4 tbsp of the oil, dripping
or butter over a medium-high heat until very hot, but not smoking.
Add the potatoes and cook for 2 minutes without stirring so that they
seal completely and brown on one side.

4 Shake the pan and toss the potatoes to brown on another side and
continue to stir and shake the pan until potatoes are evenly browned
on all sides. Season with salt and pepper.

5 Add a little more oil, dripping or butter, reduce the heat to medium-low
to low, and continue cooking the potatoes for 20–25 minutes until
tender when pierced with a knife, stirring and shaking the pan frequently.

6 About 5 minutes before the end of cooking, sprinkle the potatoes with
the chopped rosemary. Serve at once.

meat & poultry dishes

tex-mex baked potatoes with chilli

CLASSIC **CHILLI MINCE** TOPS CRISP, FLOURY-CENTRED BAKED POTATOES. **EASY** TO PREPARE AND GREAT FOR A SIMPLE, YET **SUBSTANTIAL** FAMILY SUPPER.

method

SERVES 4

1 Preheat the oven to 220°C/425°F/Gas 7. Brush or rub the potatoes with a little of the oil and then pierce them with skewers.

2 Place the potatoes on the top shelf of the oven and bake them for 30 minutes before beginning to cook the chilli.

3 Heat the oil in a large heavy pan and add the garlic, onion and pepper. Fry gently for 4–5 minutes until softened.

4 Add the beef and fry until browned, then stir in the chilli, cumin, cayenne pepper, tomatoes, tomato paste, 60ml/4 tbsp water and the herbs. Bring to a boil, then reduce the heat, cover and simmer for about 25 minutes, stirring occasionally.

5 Stir in the kidney beans and cook, uncovered, for 5 minutes. Remove from the heat and stir in the chopped coriander. Season well and set aside.

6 Cut the baked potatoes in half and place them in serving bowls. Top with the chilli mixture and a dollop of soured cream. Garnish with chopped fresh marjoram and serve hot accompanied by a few lettuce leaves.

ingredients

2 large **baking potatoes**
15ml/1 tbsp **vegetable oil**, plus more for brushing
1 **garlic clove**, crushed
1 small **onion**, chopped
1/2 **red pepper**, seeded and chopped
225g/8oz lean **beef mince**
1/2 small fresh **red chilli**, seeded and chopped
5ml/1 tsp ground **cumin**
pinch of **cayenne pepper**
200g/7oz can chopped **tomatoes**
30ml/2 tbsp **tomato paste**
2.5ml/1/2 tsp fresh **oregano**
2.5ml/1/2 tsp fresh **marjoram**
200g/7oz can red **kidney beans**, drained
15ml/1 tbsp chopped fresh **coriander**
salt and ground **black pepper**
chopped fresh **marjoram**, to garnish
lettuce leaves, to serve
60ml/4 tbsp **soured cream**, to serve

THIS IS REAL **NURSERY** OR COMFORT FOOD AT ITS **BEST**. WHETHER YOU REMEMBER GRAN'S VERSION, OR PREFER THIS **AMERICAN-STYLE** HASH, IT TURNS CORNED BEEF INTO A **SUPPER** FIT FOR ANY GUEST.

ingredients

30ml/2 tbsp **vegetable oil**

25g/1oz/2 tbsp **butter**

1 **onion**, finely chopped

1 **green pepper**, seeded and diced

2 large firm boiled **potatoes**, diced

350g/12oz can **corned beef**, cubed

1.5ml/¼ tsp grated **nutmeg**

1.5ml/¼ tsp **paprika**

4 **eggs**

salt and ground **black pepper**

deep-fried **parsley**, to garnish

sweet chilli sauce or **tomato sauce**, to serve

corned beef & egg hash

method

SERVES 4

1 Heat the oil and butter together in a large frying pan. Add the onion and fry for 5–6 minutes until softened.

2 In a bowl, mix together the green pepper, potatoes, corned beef, nutmeg and paprika and season well. Add to the pan and toss gently to distribute the cooked onion.

3 Press down lightly and fry without stirring on a medium heat for about 3–4 minutes until a golden brown crust has formed on the underside. Stir the mixture through to distribute the crust, then repeat the frying twice, until the mixture is well browned.

4 Make four wells in the hash and carefully crack an egg into each. Cover and cook gently for about 4–5 minutes until the egg whites are set.

5 Sprinkle with deep fried parsley and cut into quarters. Serve hot with sweet chilli or tomato sauce.

cook's tip
Put the can of corned beef into the fridge to chill for about half an hour before using – it will firm up and cut into cubes more easily.

steak with stout & potatoes

THE **IRISH** WAY TO BRAISE BEEF IS IN **STOUT** OF COURSE, TOPPED WITH **THICKLY SLICED** POTATOES. BAKE IT IN A MODERATE OVEN FOR LONG, SLOW **TENDERIZING** IF YOU PREFER.

ingredients

675g/1½lb **stewing beef**
15ml/1 tbsp **vegetable oil**
25g/1oz/2 tbsp **butter**
225g/8oz tiny **white onions**
175ml/6fl oz/¾ cup **stout** or
   dark beer
300ml/½ pint/1¼ cups **beef**
   stock
bouquet garni
675g/1½lb firm, **waxy**
   potatoes, cut into thick slices
225g/8oz/3 cups large
   mushrooms, sliced
15ml/1 tbsp **plain flour**
2.5ml/½ tsp mild **mustard**
salt and ground **black pepper**
chopped **thyme sprigs**, to
   garnish

variation
For a dish that is lighter, but just as tasty, substitute 4 lamb leg steaks for the beef, and use dry cider instead of the stout or beer, and lamb or chicken stock instead of beef.

method
SERVES 4

1 Trim any excess fat from the steak and cut into four pieces. Season both sides of the meat. Heat the oil and 10g/¼oz/1½ tsp of the butter in a large heavy-based pan.

2 Add the steak and brown on both sides, taking care not to burn the butter. Remove from the pan and set aside.

3 Add the tiny white onions to the pan and cook for 3–4 minutes until lightly browned all over. Return the steak to the pan with the onions. Pour on the stout or beer and stock and season the whole mixture to taste.

4 Next add the bouquet garni to the pan and top with the potato slices, distributing them evenly over the surface to cover the steak. Bring the ingredients to the boil, then reduce the heat, cover with a tight-fitting lid and simmer gently for 1 hour.

5 Add the sliced mushrooms over the potatoes. Cover again and simmer for a further 30 minutes or so. Remove the steak and vegetables with a slotted spoon and arrange on a platter.

6 Mix the remaining butter with the flour to make a roux. Whisk a little at a time into the cooking liquid in the pan. Stir in the mustard. Cook over a medium heat for 2–3 minutes, stirring all the while, until thickened.

7 Season the sauce and pour over the steak. Garnish with plenty of thyme sprigs and serve the dish at once.

cook's tip
To make onion peeling easier, first put the onions in a bowl and cover with boiling water. Allow them to soak for about 5 minutes and drain. The skins should now peel away easily.

YOU WILL FIND NUMEROUS VARIATIONS OF THIS **TRADITIONAL** SUPPER DISH THROUGHOUT **IRELAND**, BUT THE BASIC INGREDIENTS ARE THE SAME WHEREVER YOU GO – **POTATOES**, **SAUSAGES** AND **BACON**.

ingredients

15ml/1 tbsp **vegetable oil**, plus extra for greasing

4 **bacon** rashers, cut into 2.5cm/1in pieces

2 large **onions**, chopped

2 **garlic cloves**, crushed

8 large **pork sausages**

4 large **baking potatoes**, thinly sliced

1.5ml/¼ tsp fresh **sage**

300ml/½ pint/1¼ cups **vegetable stock**

salt and ground **black pepper**

soda bread, to serve

potato & sausage casserole

method

SERVES 4–6

1 Preheat the oven to 180°C/350°F/ Gas 4. Grease a large ovenproof dish with some of the oil and set aside.

2 Heat the oil in a frying pan. Add the bacon and fry for 2 minutes.

3 Add the onions and fry for 5–6 minutes until golden. Add the garlic and fry for 1 minute, then remove the mixture from the pan and set aside.

4 Then fry the sausages in the pan for 5–6 minutes until golden brown.

5 Arrange the potatoes in the base of the prepared dish. Spoon the bacon and onion mixture on top. Season with the salt and pepper and sprinkle with the fresh sage.

6 Pour on the stock and top with the sausages. Cover and bake for 1 hour. Serve hot with fresh soda bread.

pork escalopes baked with apple & potato rösti

THE **JUICES** FROM THE PORK COOK INTO THE APPLES AND POTATOES GIVING THEM A WONDERFUL **FLAVOUR** AS WELL AS MAKING A DELICIOUS **SAUCE**.

method

SERVES 4

1 Preheat the oven to 200°C/400°F/Gas 6. Squeeze out all the excess liquid from the grated potatoes and apple. Mix the grated ingredients together with the garlic, egg and seasoning.

2 Divide the potatoes into 4 portions and spoon each quarter on to a baking sheet that has been lined with foil and greased. Form a circle with the potatoes and flatten out slightly with the back of a spoon. Drizzle with a little olive oil. Cook for 10 minutes.

3 Meanwhile, lay the Parma ham on a clean surface and place a pork escalope on top. Lay a sage leaf and apple wedges over each escalope and top each piece with the butter. Wrap the Parma ham around each piece of meat, making sure it is covered completely.

4 Remove the potatoes from the oven, place each pork parcel on top and return to the oven for 20 minutes. Carefully lift the pork and potatoes off the foil and serve with caramelized wedges of apple and any cooking juices on the side.

---

cook's tip

Do not be tempted to overcook the pork as it will start to dry out.

ingredients

2 large **potatoes**, finely grated

1 medium **Bramley apple**, grated

2 **garlic cloves**, crushed

1 **egg**, beaten

butter, for greasing

15ml/1 tbsp **olive oil**

4 large slices **Parma ham**

4 **pork escalopes**, about 175g/6oz each

4 **sage** leaves

1 medium **Bramley apple**, cut into thin wedges

25g/1oz/2 tbsp **butter**, diced

salt and ground **black pepper**

caramelized **apple wedges**, to serve

irish stew

method

SERVES 6–8

SIMPLE AND DELICIOUS, THIS IS THE QUINTESSENTIAL IRISH MAIN COURSE. TRADITIONALLY MUTTON CHOPS ARE USED, BUT AS THEY ARE HARDER TO FIND THESE DAYS YOU CAN USE LAMB INSTEAD.

ingredients

1.2kg/2½lb boneless **lamb chops**

15ml/1 tbsp **vegetable oil**

3 large **onions**, quartered

4 large **carrots**, thickly sliced

900ml/1½ pints/3¾ cups **water**

4 large firm **potatoes**, cut into chunks

1 large **thyme sprig**

15g/½oz/1 tbsp **butter**

15ml/1 tbsp chopped fresh **parsley**

salt and ground **black pepper**

Savoy cabbage, to serve

cook's tip

If you can't find boneless chops, use the same weight of middle neck of lamb. Ask the butcher to chop the meat into cutlets, which should then be trimmed of excess fat.

1 Trim any excess fat from the lamb. Heat the oil in a flameproof casserole, add the lamb and brown on both sides. Remove from the pan.

2 Add the onions and carrots to the casserole and cook for 5 minutes until the onions are browned. Return the lamb to the pan with the water. Season with salt and pepper. Bring to a boil, then reduce the heat, cover and simmer for 1 hour.

3 Add the potatoes to the pan with the thyme, cover again, and simmer for a further hour.

4 Leave the stew to settle for a few minutes. Remove the fat from the liquid with a ladle, then pour off the liquid into a clean saucepan. Bring to a simmer and stir in the butter, then the parsley. Season well and pour back into the casserole. Serve with Savoy cabbage, boiled or steamed, if liked.

middle eastern roast lamb & potatoes

method

SERVES 6–8

WHEN THE EASTERN AROMA OF THE GARLIC AND SAFFRON COME WAFTING OUT OF THE OVEN, THIS DELICIOUSLY GARLICKY LAMB WON'T LAST VERY LONG!

ingredients

2.75kg/6lb **leg of lamb**

4 **garlic cloves**, halved

60ml/4 tbsp **olive oil**

juice of 1 **lemon**

2–3 **saffron** strands, soaked in 15ml/1 tbsp boiling **water**

5ml/1 tsp **mixed dried herbs**

450g/1lb **baking potatoes**, thickly sliced

2 large **onions**, thickly sliced

salt and ground **black pepper**

fresh **thyme**, to garnish

1 Make eight incisions in the lamb, press the garlic into the slits and place the lamb in a non-metallic dish.

2 Mix together the oil, lemon juice, saffron mixture and herbs. Rub over the lamb and marinate for 2 hours.

3 Preheat the oven to 180°C/350°F/Gas 4. Layer the potatoes and onions in a large roasting tin. Lift the lamb out of the marinade and place the lamb on top of the potatoes and onions, fat side up and season.

4 Pour any remaining marinade over the lamb and roast for 2 hours, basting occasionally. Remove from the oven, cover with foil and rest for 10–15 minutes before carving. Garnish with thyme.

chicken with potato dumplings

POACHED CHICKEN BREAST IN A CREAMY
SAUCE TOPPED WITH **LIGHT** HERB AND
POTATO DUMPLINGS MAKES A **DELICATE**
YET HEARTY AND **WARMING** MEAL.

method

SERVES 4

1 Place the onion, stock and wine in a deep-sided frying pan. Add the chicken and simmer for 20 minutes, covered.

2 Remove the chicken from the stock, cut into chunks and reserve. Strain the stock and discard the onion. Reduce the stock by one-third over a high heat. Stir in the cream and tarragon and simmer until just thickened. Stir in the chicken and season with salt and ground black pepper.

3 Spoon the mixture into a 900ml/1½ pint/3¾ cup ovenproof dish.

4 Preheat the oven to 190°C/375°F/Gas 5. Mix together the dumpling ingredients and stir in the water to make a soft dough. Divide into six and shape into balls with floured hands. Place on top of the chicken mixture and bake uncovered for 30 minutes.

> ### cook's tip
> Make sure that you do not reduce the sauce too much before it is cooked in the oven as the dumplings absorb quite a lot of the liquid.

ingredients

1 **onion**, chopped
300ml/½ pint/1¼ cups
   vegetable stock
120ml/4fl oz/½ cup **white wine**
4 large **chicken breasts**
300ml/½ pint/1¼ cups **single
   cream**
15ml/1 tbsp chopped fresh
   tarragon
salt and ground **black pepper**

For the dumplings
225g/8oz main crop **potatoes**,
   boiled and mashed
175g/6oz/1¼ cups **suet**
115g/4oz/1 cup **self-raising
   flour**
30ml/2 tbsp chopped mixed
   fresh **herbs**
50ml/2fl oz/¼ cup **water**
salt and ground **black pepper**

THE **RICH** FLAVOUR OF **DUCK** COMBINED WITH THESE SWEETENED POTATOES GLAZED WITH **HONEY** MAKES AN EXCELLENT TREAT FOR A DINNER PARTY OR **SPECIAL** OCCASION.

ingredients

1 **duckling**, giblets removed

60ml/4 tbsp **light soy sauce**

150ml/¼ pint/⅔ cup fresh **orange juice**

3 large **floury potatoes**, cut into chunks

30ml/2 tbsp clear **honey**

15ml/1 tbsp **sesame seeds**

salt and ground **black pepper**

roasted duckling on a bed of honeyed potatoes

method SERVES 4

1 Preheat the oven to 200°C/400°F/Gas 6. Place the duckling in a roasting tin. Prick the skin well.

2 Mix the soy sauce and orange juice together and pour over the duck. Cook for 20 minutes.

3 Place the potato chunks in a bowl, stir in the honey and toss to mix well.

4 Remove the duckling from the oven and spoon the potatoes all around and under the duckling.

5 Roast for 35 minutes and remove from the oven. Toss the potatoes in the juices so the underside will be cooked and turn the duck over. Put back in the oven and cook for a further 30 minutes.

6 Remove the duckling from the oven and carefully scoop off the excess fat, leaving the juices behind.

7 Sprinkle the sesame seeds over the potatoes, season and turn the duckling back over, breast side up, and cook for a further 10 minutes. Remove the duckling and potatoes from the oven and keep warm, allowing the duck to stand for a few minutes.

8 Pour off the excess fat and simmer the juices on the hob for a few minutes. Serve the juices with the carved duckling and potatoes.

fish dishes

classic fish pie

ORIGINALLY A FISH PIE WAS BASED ON THE "**CATCH OF THE DAY**". NOW WE CAN CHOOSE EITHER THE FISH WE LIKE BEST, OR THE VARIETY THAT OFFERS **BEST VALUE** FOR MONEY.

method

SERVES 4

1 Preheat the oven to 220°C/425°F/Gas 7. Grease an ovenproof dish and set aside. Cut the fish into bite-size pieces. Season the fish, sprinkle over the lemon rind and place in the base of the prepared dish. Allow to sit while you make the topping.

2 Cook the potatoes in boiling salted water until tender.

3 Meanwhile make the sauce. Melt the butter in a saucepan, add the flour and cook, stirring, for a few minutes. Remove from the heat and gradually whisk in the milk. Return to the heat and bring to the boil, then reduce the heat and simmer, whisking all the time, until the sauce has thickened and achieved a smooth consistency. Add the parsley and season to taste. Pour over the fish mixture.

4 Drain the potatoes well and then mash with the butter.

5 Pipe or spoon the potatoes on top of the fish mixture. Brush the beaten egg over the potatoes. Bake for 45 minutes until the top is golden brown. Serve hot.

ingredients

butter, for greasing
450g/1lb **mixed fish**, such as cod or salmon fillets and peeled prawns
finely grated rind of 1 **lemon**
450g/1lb **floury potatoes**
25g/1oz/2 tbsp **butter**
salt and ground **black pepper**
1 **egg**, beaten

For the sauce
15g/½oz/1 tbsp **butter**
15ml/1 tbsp **plain flour**
150ml/¼ pint/⅔ cup **milk**
45ml/3 tbsp chopped fresh **parsley**

cook's tip
If using frozen fish defrost it very well first, as lots of water will ruin your pie.

NATURAL AND **SMOKED** FISH MAKE A GREAT COMBINATION, ESPECIALLY WITH THE HINT OF **TOMATO** AND **BASIL**. SERVED WITH A GREEN SALAD, IT MAKES AN **IDEAL** DISH FOR LUNCH OR A **FAMILY** SUPPER.

ingredients

1kg/2¹/4lb **smoked cod**
1kg/2¹/4lb **white cod**
900ml/1¹/2 pint/3³/4 cups **milk**
1.2 litres/2 pints/5 cups **water**
2 **basil sprigs**
1 **lemon thyme sprig**
150g/5oz/10 tbsp **butter**
1 **onion**, chopped
75g/3oz/²/3 cup **plain flour**
30ml/2 tbsp chopped fresh **basil**
4 firm **plum tomatoes**, peeled
     and chopped
12 medium main crop **floury**
     potatoes
salt and ground **black pepper**
crushed **black peppercorns**,
     to garnish
lettuce leaves, to serve

cod, basil, tomato & potato pie

method

SERVES 8

1 Place both kinds of fish in a roasting tin with 600ml/1 pint/2¹/2 cups of the milk, the water and the herb sprigs. Bring to a simmer and cook gently for about 3–4 minutes. Leave the fish to cool in the liquid for about 20 minutes. Drain the fish, reserving the cooking liquid for use in the sauce. Flake the fish, removing any skin and bone.

2 Melt 75g/3oz/6 tbsp of the butter in a large pan, add the onion and cook for about 5 minutes until softened and tender but not browned.

3 Sprinkle over the flour and half the chopped basil. Gradually add the reserved fish cooking liquid, adding a little more milk if necessary to make a fairly thin sauce, stirring constantly to make a smooth consistency. Bring to the boil, season with salt and pepper, and add the remaining basil.

4 Remove the pan from the heat, then add the fish and tomatoes and stir gently to combine. Pour into an ovenproof dish.

5 Preheat the oven to 180°C/350°F/Gas 4. Cook the potatoes in boiling water until tender. Drain, then add the remaining butter and milk, and mash. Season to taste and spoon over the fish mixture, using a fork to create a pattern. You can freeze the pie at this stage. Bake for 30 minutes until the top is golden. Sprinkle with the crushed peppercorns and serve hot with lettuce.

classic fish & chips

NOTHING BEATS A PIECE OF **COD** COOKED TO A CRISP WITH FRESHLY MADE **CHIPS** ON THE SIDE. THE BATTER SHOULD BE **LIGHT** AND CRISP, BUT NOT TOO GREASY AND THE FISH SHOULD **MELT** IN THE MOUTH. SERVE WITH **LIME WEDGES** IF YOU REALLY WANT TO TART IT UP. THE SECRETS OF COOKING FISH AND CHIPS SUCCESSFULLY ARE TO MAKE SURE THE OIL IS **FRESH AND CLEAN**. HEAT THE OIL TO THE CORRECT TEMPERATURE BEFORE COOKING THE CHIPS AND AGAIN BEFORE ADDING THE FISH. SERVE THE DISH IMMEDIATELY, WHILE STILL **CRISP** AND PIPING HOT.

ingredients

method

SERVES 4

450g/1lb **potatoes**

groundnut oil for deep fat frying

4 x 175g/6oz **cod fillets**, skinned and any tiny bones removed

For the batter

75g/3oz/⅔ cup **plain flour**

1 **egg yolk**

10ml/2 tsp **oil**

salt

lemon wedges, to garnish

---

variation

Although cod is the traditional choice for fish and chips, you can also use haddock. Rock salmon, sometimes sold as huss or dogfish, also has a good flavour. It has a central bone which cannot be removed before cooking, otherwise the pieces of fish will fall apart, but can be easily prized out once the fish is served.

---

1 Cut the potatoes into 5mm/¼in thick slices. Cut each slice again to make 5mm/¼in chips.

2 Heat the oil in a deep fat fryer to 180°C/350°F. Add the chips to the fryer and cook for 3 minutes, then remove from the pan and shake off all fat. Set to one side.

3 To make the batter, sift the flour into a bowl and add the remaining ingredients with a pinch of salt. Beat well until smooth. Set aside until ready to use.

4 Cook the chips again in the fat for a further 5 minutes or so until they are really nice and crisp. Drain on kitchen paper and season with salt. Keep hot in a low oven while you cook the pieces of fish.

5 Dip the fish into the batter, making sure they are evenly coated, and shake off any excess.

6 Carefully lower the fish into the fat and cook for 5 minutes. Drain on kitchen paper. Serve with lemon wedges and the chips.

---

cook's tip

Use fresh rather than frozen fish for the very best texture and flavour. If you have to use frozen fish, defrost it thoroughly and make sure it is dry before coating with batter.

jansson's temptation

THIS IS ONE OF **SWEDEN'S** MOST FAMOUS DISHES. LAYERED WITH **ANCHOVIES** AND **ONIONS** AND BAKED WITH **CREAM**, THE POTATOES TAKE ON A WONDERFUL FLAVOUR.

ingredients

1kg/2¼lb **potatoes**

2 very large **onions**

25g/1oz/2 tbsp **butter**, finely diced, plus extra for greasing

2–3 tins **anchovy fillets**

150ml/¼ pint/⅔ cup **single cream**

150ml/¼ pint/⅔ cup **double cream**

salt and ground **black pepper**

method

SERVES 6

1 Preheat the oven to 220°C/425°F/Gas 7. Peel the potatoes and cut into matchsticks. Slice the onions into rings.

2 Grease a 1.75 litre/3 pint/7½ cup casserole dish. Layer half the potatoes and onions in it. Drain the anchovies into a bowl, reserving the oil and lay the fillets over the potatoes, then layer the remaining potatoes and onions. Season.

3 Mix the anchovy oil and single cream together, then pour evenly over the potatoes. Dot the surface with butter.

4 Cover the potatoes with foil and tightly seal the edges. Bake for 1 hour in the oven. Remove from the oven, taste and adjust the seasoning if necessary. Pour the double cream over and serve immediately.

> ### cook's tip
> To make this recipe in individual portions, pile all the ingredients except for the double cream on to large squares of buttered foil. Gather up the edges and bring them together. Bake for 40 minutes, then complete according to the recipe.

indonesian prawns with sliced potatoes

WITH A **FRESH-TASTING** COMBINATION OF PRAWNS AND THINLY SLICED POTATOES MADE IN **INDONESIAN** STYLE WITH **SATAY** SAUCE, THIS DISH IS SURPRISINGLY **RICH** AND FILLING.

ingredients

2 large **waxy maincrop potatoes**, peeled and cut in half

120ml/4fl oz/½ cup **vegetable oil**, plus extra for greasing

1 bunch **spring onions**, finely sliced

2 **red chillies**, seeded and diced

450g/1lb peeled cooked **prawns**

45ml/3 tbsp crunchy **peanut butter**

200ml/7fl oz/scant 1 cup **coconut cream**

15ml/1 tbsp **dark soy sauce**

1 bunch chopped fresh **coriander**

salt

method

SERVES 6

1 Cook the potatoes in lightly salted boiling water for 15 minutes, until tender. Drain and, when cool enough to handle, cut into 3mm/⅛in slices. Heat the oil in a frying pan and sauté the potatoes for 10 minutes, turning occasionally until browned. Drain on kitchen paper and keep hot.

2 Drain off almost all of the oil from the pan and fry the spring onions and half the chillies in the pan for 1 minute. Add the prawns and toss for a few seconds.

3 Beat together the peanut butter, coconut cream, soy sauce and remaining chilli. Add this sauce to the prawns and cook for a further minute or two until thoroughly heated through.

4 Lightly grease a large oval platter with oil and arrange the prepared potatoes evenly around the base. Spoon the prawn mixture over until the potatoes are mostly covered over. Top with the coriander.

> ### cook's tip
> For a more luxurious version, replace the cooked, peeled prawns with fresh raw, shelled king prawns.

caribbean crab cakes

CRAB MEAT MAKES **WONDERFUL** FISH CAKES, AS EVIDENCED WITH THESE GUTSY **MORSELS**. SERVED WITH A RICH TOMATO DIP, THEY BECOME GREAT **PARTY** FOOD TOO, ON "STICKS".

method

MAKES 15

1 To make the crab cakes, mix together the crab meat, potatoes, herb seasoning, mustard, peppers, oregano and egg in a large bowl. Chill the mixture in the bowl for at least 30 minutes.

2 Meanwhile, make the tomato dip to accompany the crab cakes. Melt the butter or margarine in a small pan over a medium heat.

3 Add the onion, tomatoes and garlic and sauté for about 5 minutes until the onion is tender. Add the water, vinegar, coriander and hot chilli pepper. Bring to the boil, then reduce the heat and simmer for 10 minutes.

4 Transfer the mixture to a food processor or blender and blend to a smooth purée. Pour into a bowl. Keep warm or chill as wished.

5 Using a spoon, shape the crab into rounds and dredge with flour, shaking off the excess. Heat a little oil in a frying pan and fry, a few at a time, for 2–3 minutes on each side. Drain on kitchen paper and keep warm in a low oven while cooking the remainder.

6 Serve with the tomato dip and garnish with lime wedges, coriander sprigs and whole chillies.

ingredients

225g/8oz **white crab meat** (fresh, frozen or canned)
115g/4oz cooked **floury potatoes**, mashed
30ml/2 tbsp fresh **herb** seasoning
2.5ml/1/2 tsp **mild mustard**
2.5ml/1/2 tsp ground **black pepper**
1/2 fresh **hot chilli pepper**, finely chopped
5ml/1 tsp fresh **oregano**
1 **egg**, beaten
plain flour, for dredging
vegetable oil, for frying
lime wedges and **coriander sprigs**, to garnish
fresh whole **chilli peppers**, to garnish

For the tomato dip
15g/1/2oz/1 tbsp **butter** or **margarine**
1/2 **onion**, finely chopped
2 canned **plum tomatoes**, chopped
1 **garlic clove**, crushed
150ml/1/4 pint/2/3 cup **water**
5–10ml/1–2 tsp **malt vinegar**
15ml/1 tbsp chopped fresh **coriander**
1/2 hot fresh **chilli pepper**, chopped

THIS IS A **SIMPLE** SUPPER USING A SELECTION OF BASIC **STORE CUPBOARD** INGREDIENTS. USING **PILCHARDS** IN TOMATO SAUCE GIVES A GREATER **DEPTH** OF FLAVOUR TO THE FINISHED DISH.

ingredients

225g/8oz **potatoes**, diced

425g/15oz can **pilchards** in tomato sauce, boned and flaked

1 small **leek**, very finely diced

5ml/1 tsp **lemon juice**

salt and ground **black pepper**

For the coating

1 **egg**, beaten

75g/3oz/1½ cups fresh **white breadcrumbs**

vegetable oil, for frying

salad leaves, **cucumber** and **lemon wedges**, to garnish

mayonnaise and **bread rolls**, to serve

pilchard & leek potato cakes

method   SERVES 6

1 Cook the potatoes in lightly salted boiling water for 10 minutes or until tender. Drain, mash, and cool.

2 Add the pilchards and their tomato sauce, leek and lemon juice. Season with salt and pepper and then beat well until you have formed a smooth paste. Chill for 30 minutes.

3 Divide the mixture into six pieces and shape into cakes. For the coating, dip each cake in the egg and then the breadcrumbs.

4 Heat the oil and shallow fry the fish cakes on each side for 5 minutes. Drain on kitchen paper and garnish with salad leaves, cucumber ribbons and lemon wedges. Serve with mayonnaise on bread rolls.

vegetarian dishes

baked potatoes & three fillings

method

SERVES 4

POTATOES BAKED IN THEIR **SKINS** UNTIL THEY ARE **CRISP** ON THE OUTSIDE AND **FLUFFY** IN THE MIDDLE MAKE AN EXCELLENT AND **NOURISHING** MEAL ON THEIR OWN. BUT FOR AN EVEN BETTER **TREAT**, ADD ONE OF THESE DELICIOUS AND EASY **TOPPINGS**.

ingredients

4 medium **baking potatoes**

olive oil

sea salt

filling of your choice (see below)

1 Preheat the oven to 200°C/400°F/Gas 6. Score the potatoes with a cross and rub all over with the olive oil.

2 Place on a baking sheet and cook for 45 minutes to 1 hour until a knife inserted into their centres indicates they are cooked. Or cook in the microwave according to your manufacturer's instructions.

3 Cut the potatoes open along the score lines and push up the flesh. Season and fill with your chosen filling.

---

cook's tip

Choose potatoes that are evenly sized and have undamaged skins, and scrub them thoroughly. If they are done before you are ready to serve them, take them out of the oven and wrap them up in a warmed cloth until they are needed.

---

red bean chillies

ingredients

425g/15oz can **red kidney beans**, drained

200g/7oz/scant 1 cup low-fat **cottage** or **cream cheese**

30ml/2 tbsp **mild chilli sauce**

5ml/1 tsp ground **cumin**

method

SERVES 4

1 Heat the beans in a pan or microwave and stir in the cottage or cream cheese, chilli sauce and cumin. Serve topped with more chilli sauce.

cheese & creamy corn

ingredients

425g/15oz can **creamed corn**

115g/4oz/1 cup **hard cheese**, grated

5ml/1 tsp mixed dried **herbs**

fresh **parsley sprigs**, to garnish

method

SERVES 4

1 Heat the corn gently with the cheese and mixed herbs until well blended. Use to fill the potatoes and garnish with fresh parsley sprigs.

stir-fry veg

ingredients

45ml/3 tbsp **groundnut** or **sunflower oil**

2 **leeks**, thinly sliced

2 **carrots**, cut into sticks

1 **courgette**, thinly sliced

115g/4oz **baby corn**, halved

115g/4oz/1½ cup **button mushrooms**, sliced

45ml/3 tbsp **soy sauce**

30ml/2 tbsp **dry sherry** or **vermouth**

15ml/1 tbsp **sesame oil**

sesame seeds, to garnish

method

SERVES 4

1 Heat the groundnut or sunflower oil in a wok or large frying pan until really hot. Add the leeks, carrots, courgette and baby corn and stir-fry together for about 2 minutes, then add the mushrooms and stir-fry for a further minute.

2 Mix the soy sauce, sherry or vermouth and sesame oil and pour over the vegetables. Heat through until just bubbling and scatter the sesame seeds over.

potatoes with blue cheese & walnuts

FIRM SMALL **POTATOES**, SERVED IN A **CREAMY** BLUE CHEESE SAUCE WITH THE CRUNCH OF **WALNUTS**, MAKE A GREAT SIDE DISH. FOR A **CHANGE**, SERVE IT AS A LUNCH DISH OR A **LIGHT SUPPER** WITH A **GREEN SALAD**.

ingredients

450g/1lb small **new** or **salad potatoes**
1 small head of **celery**, sliced
1 small **red onion**, sliced
115g/4oz/1 cup **blue cheese**, mashed

150ml/1/4 pint/2/3 cup **single cream**
50g/2oz/1/2 cup **walnut** pieces
30ml/2 tbsp chopped fresh **parsley**
salt and ground **black pepper**

method

SERVES 4

1 Cook the potatoes in their skins in a large saucepan with plenty of boiling water for about 15 minutes or until tender, adding the sliced celery and onion to the pan for the last 5 minutes or so of cooking.

2 Drain the vegetables well through a colander and put them into a shallow serving dish.

3 In a small saucepan, slowly melt the cheese in the cream, stirring occasionally. Do not allow the mixture to boil but heat it until it scalds.

4 Check the sauce and season to taste. Pour it evenly over the vegetables in the dish and scatter over the walnut pieces and fresh parsley. Serve hot, straight from the dish.

> ### cook's tip
> Use a combination of blue cheeses, such as Dolcelatte and Roquefort, or go for the distinctive flavour of Stilton on its own. If walnuts are not available, blue cheeses marry equally well with hazelnuts.

raclette with new potatoes

TRADITIONAL TO BOTH **SWITZERLAND** AND **FRANCE**, RACLETTE MELTS TO A **VELVETY** CREAMINESS AND WARM **GOLDEN** COLOUR AND HAS A SAVOURY TASTE WITH A HINT OF **SWEETNESS**.

ingredients

For the pickle
2 **red onions**, sliced
5ml/1 tsp **sugar**
90ml/6 tbsp **red wine vinegar**
2.5ml/1/2 tsp **salt**
generous pinch of dried **dill**

For the potatoes
500g/11/4lb **new** or **salad potatoes**, halved if large
250g/9oz **raclette cheese** slices
salt and ground **black pepper**

method

SERVES 4

1 To make the pickle spread out the onions in a glass dish, pour over boiling water to cover and leave until cold.

2 Meanwhile mix the sugar, vinegar, salt and dill in a small pan. Heat gently, stirring, until the sugar has dissolved, then set aside to cool.

3 Drain the onions and return them to the dish, pour the vinegar mixture over, cover and leave for at least 1 hour, preferably overnight.

4 Cook the potatoes in their skins in boiling water until tender, then drain and place in a roasting tin. Preheat the grill. Season the potatoes and arrange the raclette on top. Place the tin under the grill until the cheese melts. Serve hot. Drain the excess vinegar from the red onion pickle and serve the pickle with the potatoes.

> ### cook's tip
> To speed up the process look for ready-sliced raclette for this dish. It is available from most large supermarkets and specialist cheese shops.

WRAP UP A **TASTY** MIXTURE OF VEGETABLES IN A **SPICY**, CREAMY SAUCE WITH CRISP **FILO** PASTRY. SERVE WITH A GOOD SELECTION OF **CHUTNEYS** OR A YOGURT SAUCE.

ingredients

1 **onion**, chopped

2 **carrots**, coarsely grated

1 **courgette**, chopped

350g/12oz firm **potatoes**, finely chopped

65g/2¹⁄₂ oz/5 tbsp **butter**

10ml/2 tsp mild **curry paste**

2.5ml/¹⁄₂ tsp dried **thyme**

150ml/¹⁄₄ pint/²⁄₃ cup **water**

1 **egg**, beaten

30ml/2 tbsp **single cream**

50g/2oz/¹⁄₂ cup **Cheddar cheese**, grated

8 sheets **filo pastry**, thawed if frozen

sesame seeds, for sprinkling

salt and ground **black pepper**

chutney, to serve

spicy potato strudel

method

SERVES 6

1 In a large frying pan cook the onion, carrots, courgette and potatoes in 25g/1oz/2 tbsp of the butter for 5 minutes, tossing frequently so they cook evenly. Add the curry paste and stir in. Continue to cook the vegetables for a further minute or so.

2 Add the thyme, water and seasoning. Bring to the boil, then reduce the heat and simmer for 10 minutes until tender, stirring occasionally.

3 Remove from the heat and leave to cool. Transfer the mixture to a large bowl and then mix in the egg, cream and cheese. Chill until ready to fill the filo pastry.

4 Melt the remaining butter and lay out four sheets of filo pastry, slightly overlapping them to form a fairly large rectangle. Brush with some melted butter and fit the other sheets on top. Brush again.

5 Preheat the oven to 190°C/375°F/Gas 5. Spoon the filling along one long side, then roll up the pastry. Form it into a circle and set on a baking sheet. Brush again with the last of the butter and sprinkle over the sesame seeds.

6 Bake the strudel in the oven for about 25 minutes, until golden and crisp. Stand for 5 minutes before cutting, then serve with chutney.

pepper & potato tortilla

TORTILLA IS TRADITIONALLY A **SPANISH** DISH LIKE A THICK **OMELETTE**, BEST EATEN COLD IN CHUNKY **WEDGES**. IT MAKES IDEAL PICNICKING FOOD. USE A HARD SPANISH **CHEESE**, LIKE **MAHÓN**, OR A GOAT'S CHEESE, ALTHOUGH SHARP **CHEDDAR** MAKES A GOOD SUBSTITUTE.

method

SERVES 6

1 Par-boil the potatoes in boiling water for about 10 minutes. Drain and leave to cool slightly. Slice them thickly. Preheat the grill.

2 In a large non-stick or well-seasoned frying pan, heat the oil over a medium heat. Add the onion, garlic and peppers and cook for 5 minutes until softened.

3 Add the potatoes and continue frying, stirring occasionally, until the potatoes are tender.

4 Pour in half the beaten eggs, sprinkle half the cheese over this and then the remainder of the egg. Season. Finish with a layer of cheese. Reduce the heat to low and continue to cook without stirring, half covering the pan with a lid to help set the eggs.

5 When the tortilla is firm, place the pan under the hot grill to seal the top just lightly. Leave the tortilla in the pan to cool. Serve at room temperature, cut into wedges.

ingredients

2 medium firm **potatoes**
45ml/3 tbsp **olive oil**, plus more
    if necessary
1 **large onion**, thinly sliced
2 **garlic cloves**, crushed
2 **peppers**, one green and one
    red, seeded and thinly sliced
6 **eggs**, beaten
115g/4oz/1 cup sharp **cheese**,
    grated
salt and ground **black pepper**

variation
You can add any sliced and lightly cooked vegetable, such as mushrooms, courgette or broccoli, to this tortilla instead of the green and red peppers.

potato & cabbage rissoles

THESE **TASTY** RISSOLES ARE A GREAT WAY TO MAKE USE OF ANY LEFTOVER **POTATOES** AND **CABBAGE**. THEY ARE **QUICK** TO MAKE AND **PERFECT** FOR ANY LIGHT MEAL. YOU COULD MAKE THEM FOR **BRUNCH** TEAMED WITH FRIED **EGGS**, GRILLED **TOMATOES** AND **MUSHROOMS**.

ingredients

450g/1lb **mashed potato**
225g/8oz steamed or boiled
   cabbage or **kale**, shredded
1 **egg**, beaten
115g/4oz/1 cup **Cheddar**
   cheese, grated

freshly grated **nutmeg**
plain flour, for coating
vegetable oil, for frying
salt and ground **black pepper**
lettuce, to serve

method

SERVES 4

1 Mix the potato with the cabbage or kale, egg, cheese, nutmeg and seasoning. Divide and shape into eight small sausage shapes.

2 Chill for an hour or so, if possible, as this enables the rissoles to become firm and makes them easier to fry. Dredge them in the flour, shaking off the excess.

3 Heat a 1cm/½ in layer of oil in a frying pan until it is really hot. Carefully slide the rissoles into the oil and fry in batches on each side for about 3 minutes until golden and crisp.

4 Remove the rissoles from the pan and drain on kitchen paper. Serve piping hot with fresh lettuce leaves.

---

cook's tip

If you want to flavour the rissoles with a stronger tasting cheese, try a blue, such as Stilton or Shropshire Blue.

---

potato, mozzarella & garlic pizza

NEW POTATOES, **SMOKED MOZZARELLA** AND **GARLIC** MAKE THIS PIZZA UNIQUE. YOU COULD ADD SLICED **MUSHROOMS** OR **PEPPERS** TO MAKE IT AN EVEN MORE SUBSTANTIAL MEAL.

ingredients

350g/12oz small **new** or
   salad potatoes
45ml/3 tbsp **olive oil**
2 **garlic cloves**, crushed
1 **pizza base**, 25–30cm/
   10–12 in diameter
1 **red onion**, thinly sliced

150g/5oz/1¼ cups **smoked**
   mozzarella cheese, grated
10ml/2 tsp chopped **fresh**
   rosemary or **sage**
salt and ground **black pepper**
30ml/2 tbsp freshly grated
   Parmesan cheese, to garnish

method

SERVES 4

1 Preheat the oven to 220°C/425°F/Gas 7. Cook the potatoes in boiling salted water for 5 minutes. Drain well and leave to cool. Peel and slice thinly.

2 Heat 30ml/2 tbsp of the oil in a frying pan. Add the sliced potatoes and garlic and fry for 5–8 minutes turning frequently until tender.

3 Brush the pizza base with the remaining oil. Scatter the onion over, then arrange the potatoes on top.

4 Sprinkle over the mozzarella and rosemary or sage and plenty of black pepper. Bake for 15–20 minutes until golden. Remove from the oven, sprinkle with Parmesan and more black pepper.

potato & pumpkin gnocchi with a chanterelle parsley cream

ITALIANS LOVE **PUMPKIN** AND OFTEN INCORPORATE IT INTO THEIR **DUMPLINGS** AND OTHER **TRADITIONAL** PASTA DISHES AS IT ADDS A SLIGHT **SWEET RICHNESS**. THE COMBINATION OF **POTATO** AND **PUMPKIN** MAKES THIS A **FLAVOURSOME**, SATISFYING MEAL.

ingredients

450g/1lb **floury potatoes**
450g/1lb **pumpkin**, peeled, seeded and chopped
2 **egg yolks**
200g/7oz/1¾ cups **plain flour**, plus more if necessary
pinch of ground **allspice**
1.5ml/¼ tsp **cinnamon**
pinch of freshly grated **nutmeg**
finely grated rind of ½ **orange**
salt and **ground pepper**

For the sauce
30ml/2 tbsp **olive oil**
1 **shallot**, finely chopped
175g/6oz/2½ cups fresh **chanterelles**, sliced, or 15g/½oz/½ cup dried, soaked in warm water for 20 minutes, then drained
10ml/2 tsp **almond butter**
150ml/¼ pint/⅔ cup **crème fraîche**
a little **milk** or **water**
75ml/5 tbsp chopped fresh **parsley**
50g/2oz/½ cup **Parmesan cheese**, freshly grated

method

SERVES 4

1 Cook the potatoes in a large saucepan of boiling salted water for 20 minutes. Drain and set aside.

2 Place the pumpkin in a bowl, cover and microwave on full power for 8 minutes. Alternatively, wrap the pumpkin in foil and bake at 180ºC/350ºF/Gas 4 for 30 minutes. Drain well.

3 Pass the pumpkin and potatoes through a food mill into a bowl. Add the egg yolks, flour, spices, orange rind and seasoning and mix well to make a soft dough. If you find that the mixture is too loose you can add a little more flour to stiffen it up.

4 Bring a large pan of salted water to a fast boil. Meanwhile, spread a layer of flour on a clean work surface. Spoon the prepared gnocchi mixture into a piping bag fitted with a 1cm/½in plain nozzle.

5 Pipe directly on to the flour to make a 15cm/6in sausage. Roll in flour and cut crossways into 2.5cm/1in pieces. Repeat to make more sausage shapes and pieces. Mark each lightly with the tines of a fork and drop into the boiling water. When they rise to the surface, after 3–4 minutes, they are done.

6 Meanwhile make the sauce. Heat the oil in a non-stick frying pan, add the shallot and fry until soft but not coloured. Add the chanterelles and cook briefly, then add the almond butter. Stir to melt and stir in the crème fraîche. Simmer briefly and adjust the consistency with milk or water. Add the parsley and season to taste.

7 Lift the gnocchi out of the water with a slotted spoon, drain well, and turn into bowls. Spoon the sauce over the top, sprinkle with grated Parmesan, and serve at once.

variation

Turn these gnocchi into a main meal for vegetarians by serving them with a rich home-made tomato sauce. If you want to make the dish more special, serve the gnocchi with a side dish of ratatouille made from courgettes, peppers and aubergines, cooked gently with tomatoes, plenty of garlic and really good extra virgin olive oil.

cook's tip

If planning ahead, gnocchi can be shaped, ready for cooking, up to 8 hours in advance. Almond butter is available from health food shops.

breads & scones

AN **INTERESTING** COMBINATION OF **CRANBERRIES** WITH BACON AND POTATOES. THE CRANBERRIES **COLOUR** THE BREAD SLICES, GIVING IT A VERY **FESTIVE** FEEL.

ingredients

450g/1lb/4 cups **strong white flour**

5ml/1 tsp easy-blend **dried yeast**

5ml/1 tsp **salt**

25g/1oz/2 tbsp **butter**, diced

325ml/11fl oz/1⅓ cups lukewarm **water**

75g/3oz/¾ cup fresh or frozen **cranberries**, thawed

oil, for greasing

225g/8oz **floury potatoes**, halved

6 rashers rindless **streaky bacon**, chopped

30ml/2 tbsp runny **honey**

salt and ground **black pepper**

savoury cranberry & potato bread slice

method

SERVES 4

1 Sift the flour into a bowl, stir in the yeast and 5ml/1 tsp salt. Rub in the butter to form breadcrumbs. Make a well in the centre and stir in the water.

2 Bring the mixture together with a round-bladed knife and then turn out on to a floured surface. Knead for 5 minutes. Place the dough in a bowl and cover with a damp cloth. Leave to rise for 1 hour or until doubled in size.

3 Turn the dough out and knock back to remove the air bubbles. Knead for a few minutes. Carefully knead the cranberries into the bread.

4 Roll the dough out to a rectangle and place in an oiled 23 x 23cm/ 9 x 9in flan tin. Push the dough into the corners and cover with a damp cloth. Leave to rise in a warm place for 30 minutes.

5 Preheat the oven to 220°C/425°F/Gas 7. Meanwhile, boil the potatoes in plenty of salted water for 15 minutes or until just tender. Drain and when cool enough to handle, slice thinly.

6 Scatter the potatoes and bacon over the risen bread dough, season, then drizzle with the honey and bake for 25 minutes, covering the bread loosely with foil after 20 minutes to prevent burning.

7 Remove the bread from the oven and transfer to a wire rack. Return to the oven for 5 minutes to crisp the base. Leave to cool on the wire rack.

---

cook's tip
If you can't find fresh or frozen cranberries, substitute them with sweetcorn niblets.

---

three herb potato scones

THESE **FLAVOURSOME** SCONES ARE PERFECT SERVED WARM AND SPLIT IN TWO WITH HAND-CARVED **HAM** AND **PARMESAN** SHAVINGS AS A FILLING.

method

MAKES 12

1 Preheat the oven to 180°C/350°F/Gas 4. Sift the flour into a bowl with the baking powder. Add a pinch of salt. Rub in the butter with your fingertips to form crumbs. Place the potato flakes in bowl and pour over 200ml/7fl oz/scant 1 cup boiling water. Beat well and cool slightly.

2 Stir the potatoes into the dry ingredients with the herbs and milk.

3 Bring the mixture together to form a soft dough. Turn out on to a floured surface and knead the dough very gently for a few minutes, until soft and pliable.

4 Roll the dough out on a floured surface to about 4cm/1½in thickness and stamp out rounds using a 7.5cm/3in cutter. Reshape any remaining dough and re-roll for more scones. Place the scones on to a greased baking dish and brush the surfaces with a little more milk.

5 Cook for 15–20 minutes and serve warm. They can be eaten plain, or with a filling, served with apple and garnished with celery leaves.

---

cook's tip

Don't be tempted to overseason the mixture, as once cooked the baking powder can also increase the salty flavour of the finished scone and this can overpower the taste of the herbs.

ingredients

225g/8oz/2 cups **self-raising flour**
5ml/1 tsp **baking powder**
pinch of **salt**
50g/2oz/4 tbsp **butter**, diced
25g/1oz **potato flakes**
15ml/1 tbsp chopped fresh **parsley**
15ml/1 tbsp chopped fresh **basil**
15ml/1 tbsp chopped fresh **oregano**
150ml/¼ pint/⅔ cup **milk**
oil, for greasing
apple wedges, to serve
celery leaves, to garnish

grated cheese & onion potato bread

A **PLAITED LOAF** WITH A CRISP CHEESE AND ONION TOPPING. IDEALLY YOU SHOULD SERVE THIS BREAD BY PULLING **CHUNKS** OFF THE LOAF RATHER THAN SLICING, SO THAT YOU GET MASSES OF **TOPPING** WITH EACH BITE. THIS BREAD IS PARTICULARLY **DELICIOUS** SERVED WARM.

ingredients

225g/8oz **floury potatoes**

350g/12oz/3 cups **strong white flour**

7.5ml/1½ tsp easy-blend **dried yeast**

25g/1oz/2 tbsp **butter**, diced

50g/2oz/½ cup pitted green or black **olives**

salt and ground **black pepper**

For the topping

30ml/2 tbsp **olive oil**

1 **onion**, sliced into rings

50g/2oz/½ cup mature **Cheddar cheese**, grated

cook's tip

To plait a loaf successfully, lay the three lengths of dough side by side. Plait the dough from one end to the centre and repeat with the other end. This will give an even loaf with a professional looking touch to it.

method

SERVES 4

1 Chop the potatoes and cook in a large saucepan with plenty of salted boiling water for 15–20 minutes or until tender.

2 Meanwhile, sift the flour into a bowl, add the yeast and a little salt. Rub in the butter to form fine crumbs. Drain the potatoes and mash well. Add to the dry ingredients with 300ml/½ pint/1¼ cups lukewarm water.

3 Bring the mixture together with a round-bladed knife and then turn out on to a floured surface. Knead for about 5 minutes. Return the dough to a bowl and cover with a damp cloth. Leave to rise for 1 hour or until doubled in size. Turn the dough out onto a floured surface and knock back to remove any air bubbles. Carefully knead in the olives. Cut the dough into three even pieces.

4 Roll each piece out to a long thick sausage. Twist the sausages over each other to form a plait (see Cook's Tip). Lift on to a greased baking sheet. Cover with a damp cloth and leave to rise for 30 minutes or until doubled in size.

5 Meanwhile, for the topping, preheat the oven to 220°C/425°F/Gas 7. Heat the oil in a saucepan and fry the onions for 10 minutes until they are golden.

6 Remove the onions from the pan and drain on kitchen paper.

7 Scatter the onions and grated cheese over the bread and bake in the oven for 20 minutes.

A WONDERFUL
BRUNCH DISH,
AND COMPLETELY
DELICIOUS SERVED
WITH **CRISPY BACON**.

ingredients

1 medium **sweet potato**

5ml/1 tsp ground **cinnamon**

450g/1lb/4 cups **strong white flour**

5ml/1 tsp easy-blend **dried yeast**

50g/2oz/1/2 cup **walnut** pieces

300ml/1/2 pint/11/4 cups warmed **milk**

oil, for greasing

salt and ground **black pepper**

cook's tip

For an extra-crispy loaf, after the bread is cooked, remove from the tin and return the bread to the oven placing it upside down on the oven rack. Continue to cook for a further 5 minutes.

sweet potato bread with cinnamon & walnuts

method

MAKES A 900G/2LB LOAF

1 Boil the whole potato in its skin for 45 minutes or until tender.

2 Meanwhile, sift the cinnamon and flour together into a large bowl. Stir in the dried yeast.

3 Drain the potatoes and cool in cold water, then peel the skins. Mash the potatoes with a fork and mix into the dry ingredients with the nuts.

4 Make a well in the centre and pour in the milk. Bring the mixture together with a round-bladed knife, place on to a floured surface and knead for 5 minutes.

5 Return the dough to a bowl and cover with a damp cloth. Leave to rise for 1 hour or until doubled in size. Turn the dough out and knock back to remove any air bubbles. Knead again for a few minutes. If the dough feels sticky add more flour to the mixture. Shape into a ball and place the bread in an oiled and base-lined 900g/2lb loaf tin. Cover with a damp cloth and leave to rise in a warm place for 1 hour or until doubled in size.

6 Preheat the oven to 200°C/400°F/Gas 6. Bake on the middle shelf of the oven for 25 minutes. Turn out and tap the base; if it sounds hollow the bread is cooked. Cool on a wire rack.

sweet potato scones

THESE ARE **SCONES** WITH A **DIFFERENCE**. A SWEET POTATO GIVES THEM A **PALE ORANGE** COLOUR AND THEY ARE MELTINGLY SOFT IN THE **CENTRE**, JUST WAITING FOR A **KNOB** OF BUTTER.

method

MAKES 24

1 Preheat the oven to 230°C/450°F/Gas 8. Grease a baking sheet. Sift together the flour, baking powder and salt into a bowl. Mix in the sugar.

2 In a separate bowl, mix the mashed sweet potatoes with the milk and melted butter or margarine. Beat well to blend.

3 Add the flour to the sweet potato mixture and stir to make a dough. Turn out on to a lightly floured surface and knead until the dough is soft and pliable.

4 Roll or pat out the dough to a 1cm/1/2in thickness. Cut into rounds using a 4cm/11/2in cutter.

5 Arrange the rounds on the baking sheet. Bake for about 15 minutes until risen and lightly golden. Serve warm.

ingredients

butter, for greasing
150g/5oz/11/4 cups **plain flour**
20ml/4 tsp **baking powder**
5ml/1 tsp **salt**
15g/1/2oz/1 tbsp **soft light brown sugar**
150g/5oz mashed **sweet potatoes**
150ml/1/4 pint/2/3 cup **milk**
50g/2oz/4 tbsp **butter** or **margarine**, melted

chocolate potato cake

THIS IS A VERY **RICH**, **MOIST** CHOCOLATE CAKE, TOPPED WITH A THIN LAYER OF CHOCOLATE **ICING**. USE A GOOD-QUALITY **DARK CHOCOLATE** FOR BEST RESULTS AND SERVE WITH **WHIPPED CREAM**.

ingredients

oil, for greasing
200g/7oz/1 cup **sugar**
250g/9oz/1 cup and 2 tbsp
  butter
4 **eggs**, separated
275g/10oz **dark chocolate**
75g/3oz/3/4 cup **ground**
  almonds
165g/5 1/2 oz **mashed potato**
225g/8oz/2 cups **self-raising**
  flour
5ml/1 tsp **cinnamon**
45ml/3 tbsp **milk**
white and **dark chocolate**
  shavings, to garnish
whipped cream, to serve

cook's tip
Chocolate can be melted very successfully in the microwave. Place the pieces of chocolate in a plastic measuring jug or bowl. The chocolate may scorch if placed in a glass bowl. Microwave on high for 1 minute, stir, and then heat again for up to 1 minute, checking halfway through to see if it is done.

method

MAKES A 23CM/9IN CAKE

1 Preheat the oven to 180ºC/350ºF/Gas 4. Grease and base-line a 23cm/9in round cake tin with a circle of baking parchment.

2 In a large bowl, cream together the sugar and 225g/8oz/1 cup of the butter until light and fluffy. Then beat the egg yolks into the creamed mixture one at a time until it is smooth and creamy.

3 Finely chop or grate 175g/6oz of the chocolate and stir it into the creamed mixture with the ground almonds. Pass the mashed potato through a sieve or ricer and stir it into the creamed chocolate mixture.

4 Sift together the flour and cinnamon and fold into the mixture with the milk.

5 Whisk the egg whites until they hold stiff but not dry peaks, and fold into the cake mixture.

6 Spoon into the prepared tin and smooth over the top, but make a slight hollow in the middle to help keep the surface of the cake level during cooking. Bake in the oven for 1 1/4 hours until a wooden toothpick inserted in the centre comes out clean. Allow the cake to cool slightly in the tin, then turn out and cool on a wire rack.

7 Meanwhile break up the remaining chocolate into a heatproof bowl and stand it over a saucepan of hot water. Add the remaining butter in small pieces and stir well until the chocolate has melted and the mixture is smooth and glossy.

8 Peel off the lining paper and trim the top of the cake so that it is level. Smooth over the chocolate icing and allow to set. Decorate with white and dark chocolate shavings and serve with lashings of whipped cream.

index